Jen Goss & Scott Davis

Do Smoke

A modern guide to cooking and curing.

Book Co

To my Grandparents — the original foodies!
Thanks to Kirsty, my Mum, my sister Lucy, and all the strong
women who have helped keep me organised over the years.
And of course, my children, Jimmy, Honey and Jasper. — SD

To Teresa and Julian, who taught me the love of food.
And always my family, Colin, Leon and Lucy. — JG

Published by
The Do Book Company 2024
Works in Progress Publishing Ltd
thedobook.co

Text © Jen Goss & Scott Davis 2024
Text p85 © Dan Gritten 2024
Photography © Heather Birnie 2024
Illustrations p87 © Patrick Filbee 2024

The right of Jen Goss & Scott Davis
to be identified as the authors of this
work has been asserted by them in
accordance with the Copyright,
Designs and Patents Act 1988

10 9 8 7 6 5 4 3 2 1

To find out more about our company,
books and authors, please visit
thedobook.co or follow us **@dobookco**

5 per cent of our proceeds from the sale
of this book is given to The DO Lectures
to help it achieve its aim of making
positive change: thedolectures.com

Cover designed by James Victore
Book designed and set by Ratiotype

Printed and bound by OZGraf Print
on Munken, an FSC® certified paper

MIX
Paper | Supporting
responsible forestry
FSC® C163799
www.fsc.org

A CIP catalogue record for this book is
available from the British Library

ISBN 978-1-914168-36-9

Contents

Prologue

It's a good thing Marco Pierre White didn't have a bigger kitchen. In 2004, realising the Mirabelle restaurant in London didn't have enough space for a smokery, we found an empty wine cellar under the arches on Curzon Street and decided to make our own.

I was 23 years old at the time, a dyslexic lad from a small village in west Wales who didn't know my Michelin star from my Michelin tyre. But here I was — a young chef in the capital city, experiencing flavours for the first time, being shouted at continuously, and loving life.

For all the hot-headed chefs I worked for over the years, there were mentors who saw my potential. As a henchman to the head chef at Mirabelle, I cured salmon with salt and sugar, hung it on racks, lit the wood, and shut the door. Smoking food really was that simple for me — and it can be for you, too. — SD

Introduction

There is something wonderful about smoking your own food. Done well, home smoked ingredients can add a new dimension to even quite simple dishes; layers of smoke deepen the flavour and create a rich taste that stimulates the senses. But it requires a delicate balance. Too much smoke can completely ruin the dish. It will taste acrid and bitter — like burnt toast, only worse.

SCOTT: For me, slowly smoking and curing food was a welcome change of pace after years of working in kitchens where egos clashed and tempers flared. I was taught by some of the best: Gordon Ramsay, Gary Rhodes, Jean-Georges Vongerichten, and Marco Pierre White, all of whom fuelled my passion for smoking food. Hungry for more, I travelled around the British Isles, visiting artisan smokeries from Arbroath to Skibbereen. I now live a slightly quieter (but no less busy!) life with my partner and three children in Carmarthen, Wales, where we run a bespoke catering company.

JEN: What made me so excited about smoking was how simple it was. Often in life, we assume something must be complicated because we don't know how to do it. But with food, I've found the opposite to be true — it's easy when you understand it; you just have to give it a go.

I grew up in Cardiff in a house where everything was made from scratch and food was really important. In the eighties, my parents were ahead of the curve, always experimenting with new flavours before they became mainstream. I vividly remember my first taste of pesto, eagerly scooping it with a teaspoon straight from the jar because it was so good.

I've worked in hospitality since my early twenties, both in management and in the kitchen. In 2010, I moved from London to west Wales with my young family, following a lifelong dream to live by the sea and work on the land. Now, everything I grow and forage in the surrounding hedgerows provides ample supplies for Our Two Acres — the catering company I set up and now run.

During that same year, Scott and I were both working at Llys Meddyg, a hotel and restaurant in Newport, Wales, and he taught me how to do a simple hot smoke in the kitchen. We made hot smoked trout using Lapsang Souchong (a black tea that has been smoked over pine, giving it a smoky flavour and aroma). I've used the recipe Scott taught me many times — I even cooked it at The DO Lectures, the annual event held in west Wales, for 200 people in 2017. That recipe is in this book (see page 50); you should try it and see what happens.

The origins of smoking

Smoking food dates back thousands of years. Ancient Egyptians, Greeks and Romans used it as a preserving method to extend the shelf life and enhance the flavour of meat, fish and other perishable foods. Smoking food evolved in different cultures and countries: in China, they smoked over rice and tea in a wok, and in America they would smoke over burning corn cobs. The practice declined with the introduction of fridges and chemical preservatives in the 20th century.

These days it's more about taste than necessity. But flavour aside, there are other benefits to smoking food in our modern homes.

Why smoke?

Better quality, less expensive
One of the best things about smoking your own food is that you no longer need to buy smoked food products because you know you can make it yourself, exactly how you like it, for a fraction of the price. Smoking food at home will always be better quality than anything you're going to buy in the supermarket. Sadly some cheaper smoked products haven't been near a smoker; it's just chemicals creating the smoked flavour.

We all have different palates
By doing your own smoking you can make things as smoky as you like. As such, there is always an element of trial and error until you find what works for you.

The satisfaction of learning a skill
In the same way that making sourdough or growing your own vegetables is good for your wellbeing, we all now know that slowing down, using our hands and taking time over something is beneficial to our physical and mental health.

Making the vegetable the main event
Smoking food allows you to turn the vegetable into the main event, which, in a world where many of us are eating less meat, is exciting. When thinking about smoked foods, smoked salmon or bacon often come to mind, so vegetarians or vegans might not think it's for them. But we're here to show you that it is.

Smokeries

There are a number of incredible long-standing smokeries across the British Isles that you can visit, see the smoking in action and buy smoked produce. Here are some of our favourites:

— Severn & Wye Smokery, Gloucestershire, England
— Secret Smokehouse, London, England
— Salt + Smoke, Pembrokeshire, Wales
— Belvelly Smoke House, Cork, Ireland
— Woodcock Smokery, West Cork, Ireland
— Gubbeen Smokehouse, Cork, Ireland

What to expect

In this book, you will find good ingredients, simple processes and delicious food. We will cover everything from hot and cold smoking techniques (and what that even means) to the different types of wood you can use, and the importance of preparation: brining and curing your food to get it ready for smoking.

Whether you're smoking in your kitchen or outdoor space, we'll guide you through smoking methods for meat, fish, vegetables and dairy — along with some vegan alternatives. And we'll encourage you to have a go with some recipes ranging from the 'nice and easy' to the slightly more 'sleeves rolled up'.

It will require attention to detail, experimentation and a generous helping of patience. But you can have fun smoking your own food — and believe us, you will.

Before we get started

There is a common misconception that smoking food is an out-of-reach endeavour. So let's get this clear: the process is simple. But, be warned! It's not going to be perfect the first time. It's an experiment. So take the pressure off, relax your shoulders and enjoy it. The good news is you don't even need to leave your house to start. You'll find you have most of the basic equipment in your kitchen already. But first...

Health and safety
Smoking food is very low risk as you're creating smoke, not starting a fire. But as you will be cooking in a slightly different way, we'd recommend taking precautions.

Here are some things to keep in mind:

— Always keep a fire extinguisher or bucket of water close by. You're unlikely to need it when smoking food at home, but it's better to have one than not.

— If you hot smoke food over a fire outside (using a rack with the food sealed in aluminium foil), position it (and yourself) away from anything that could catch alight and check the wind before you start.

— When using a gas hob or smoking food over an open flame, monitor it closely and avoid leaving it unattended.

Hygiene

It's essential to practise safe handling, cooking and cleaning while smoking food. For a hot smoke, always monitor the temperature of your food using a thermometer to ensure it's safe for consumption. For a cold smoke, make sure your smoker stays below 25°C (77°F), otherwise you run the risk of cooking the food. You must brine or cure high-risk foods like meat and fish first (see Chapter 2). The salt in brine dehydrates the meat or fish and the bacteria present in food (which causes it to spoil over time). Sugar also acts as a preservative by stopping the growth of bacteria. It's really important to get this bit right if you are smoking to preserve your food.

Wash your hands thoroughly with soap and water before touching any food, especially raw ingredients. Always keep raw and cooked foods separate to avoid cross-contamination (use separate chopping boards, utensils and plates). When you've finished smoking, clean and sanitise all surfaces, utensils and equipment. Dispose of any leftover wood chippings or dust and clean out the smoker to prevent any build-up of residue.

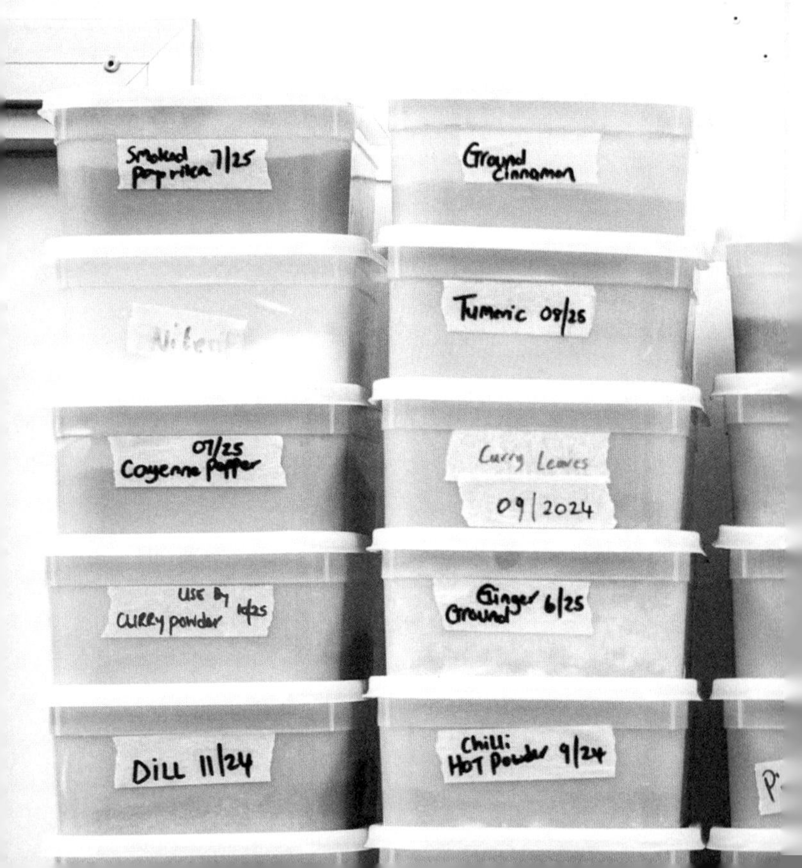

Smoked 7/25
paprika

Ground
Cinnamon

Nilenni

Tummic 09/25

07/25
Cayenne pepper

Curry Leaves
09/2024

USE BY
CURRY powder 10/25

Ginger 6/25
Ground

DILL 11/24

Chilli
HOT Powder 9/24

P.

1
The difference between hot and cold smoking — and what you'll need

There are two ways to smoke food:
hot and cold.

Hot smoking

Hot smoking is when you expose food to smoke and heat simultaneously in a controlled environment, so it both cooks and smokes the food. Hot smoking uses temperatures ranging from 82°c to 90°c (180°F to 194°F) to allow the food to absorb the smoky flavours while it is being cooked. It is typically a quicker process than cold smoking. Before you smoke meat and fish you need to brine it and generally, we would use a wet brine before hot smoking (more on that later).

General kit
For the most basic *hot* smoke, you will need:

— **Baking tray:** a sturdy rectangular baking tray will work best. A roasting tin or cheap paella pan will also do the trick.

— **Cooling rack:** choose a cooling rack that fits neatly into the baking tray.

— **Strong foil:** go for extra thick / heavy duty aluminium foil if you can. The stronger, the better.

— **Heat source:** gas hob or enclosed barbecue.

— **Meat thermometer:** for hot smoking meat (as you are cooking it at the same time), you'll want a reliable meat thermometer that accurately gauges the temperature of the meat as it cooks.

Alternatively — for smoking enthusiasts — you can invest in a hot smoker. Scott uses an Onlyfire pellet grill and smoker; other brands to look at include Masterbuilt and THÜROS. Prices start at around £200/US$260.

Cold smoking

Cold smoking is a food preservation and flavouring method where food is exposed to smoke without heat. Unlike hot smoking, which cooks the food as it smokes, cold smoking occurs at temperatures between 10°C and 25°C (50°F and 77°F) which allows the food to absorb the smoky flavours without being cooked. The temperature is in the danger zone for bacteria to multiply, so only cured or brined products should be cold smoked. This is not the case for vegetables, fruit, dairy and nuts because they are not high-risk foods.

Cold smoking is typically a longer process and is used for fish, vegetables, cheese, cream, butter and certain meats. You can expect to cold smoke dairy and vegetables for 2–4 hours and fish and meat for 12–48 hours.

General kit

For the most basic *cold* smoke, you will need:

— **Cold smoker:** a smoker can be any container that can maintain low temperatures and proper airflow, but it will require a 'generator' to create the smoke. We both use a ProQ smoker which costs around £120/US$150, but you can have a go at building one or repurposing an old fridge or even a cardboard box (see 'How to make a cardboard box cold smoker' on page 85).

— **Smoke generator:** this is a small metal tray with a metal 'coil' that you put the wood chippings and dust into (pictured opposite). The heat from the tea light in the front corner causes the wood dust to smoke. We would recommend buying one of these as it's a useful piece of kit and not too expensive (approx. £30/US$37).

Smoking materials

Both *hot* and *cold* smoking use the following:

— **Wood (chunks, chips or dust):** a local carpenter will often sell untreated hardwood chippings or bags of wood dust. Or you can order from online smoker retailers, such as ProQ Smokers in the UK. The size and type of wood you need will depend on what you are smoking.

— **Tea leaves:** Lapsang Souchong is our favourite black tea for adding bold flavours to smoked dishes. You can also use green tea, which adds a delicate fragrant flavour, or herbal tea, which infuses your smoked food with floral notes.

— **Uncooked rice:** this helps control temperature and prevents everything from burning too harshly. The ratio of rice to wood is 1:1. Add a handful of tea for extra flavour.

Types of wood

There are many different types of wood you can use to smoke food. The amount of time that the wood smokes for is important, but the all-important flavours are up to you. The following will provide you with a good place to start:

— **Oak** is the most popular wood for smoking. It generates a moderate and steady smoke, ideal for lengthy sessions. It has a medium-strong smoky flavour that works well with just about any type of meat.

— **Beech** offers a mild, consistent smoke, suitable for longer smoking sessions. It has a subtle and slightly nutty flavour, which pairs with meat and fish without overpowering the food.

- **Apple** releases a mild and fruity smoke over a moderate duration. It adds a delicate sweetness to smoked food, complementing poultry, pork and fish.

- **Maple** produces a mild, gentle smoke over a moderate duration. It has a sweet, slightly smoky flavour with hints of caramel, best for poultry, pork and vegetables.

- **Cherry** generates a sweet smoke for a moderate duration. It infuses poultry, pork and game with a sweet and fruity flavour that adds a slightly tangy dimension to the dish.

- **Hickory** produces a strong, bold smoke relatively quickly, ideal for shorter sessions. It carries the classic flavour that most people associate with bacon and is well suited to pork, ribs, bacon and poultry.

Ok, so you've learnt a bit about the difference between hot and cold smoking, the basic kit you will need, and the various types of wood you can use — even some of the reasons why you might want to smoke food in the first place. Now we're going to guide you through one of the most important steps of the process when smoking meat and fish: brining.

The importance of brining

What is brining?

Brining is the process of soaking food in a liquid solution of salt and water (wet brine), or coating it in a mix of salt, sugar and spices (dry brine or 'cure'). Brining helps to preserve food and retain its moisture while smoking, enhancing the flavour and texture of meat and fish. Needless to say, it is really important!

It's worth noting that vegetables, dairy, eggs and nuts do not need brining. However, some vegetables benefit from a light coating in oil before smoking to help absorb the smoke.

How does brining work?

Brining, or curing, works through a process called osmosis. Osmosis is when water moves from an area of lower concentration (such as the interior of meat or fish) to an area of higher concentration (the brine) through a semi-permeable membrane (the cell walls of meat or fish).

When brining meat or fish, the higher concentration of salt in the brine draws water out from the food to balance the salt concentration. At the same time, the meat or fish absorbs the salty water along with any added flavours. This process not only enhances the flavour of the food, but the salt also relaxes the protein molecules in a process called denaturation, which leads to a juicier, more tender final product. Drawing out water dehydrates the meat or fish while the salt creates an environment in which bacteria struggle to survive, helping to preserve the product we are smoking.

Dry brining achieves similar results but without the use of water. Instead, the salt on the surface draws out moisture from the meat or fish. This moisture then dissolves the salt, forming a brine that gets reabsorbed into the food along with any seasoning.

During smoking, the absorbed brine keeps the food moist while the salt adds flavour and keeps it tender. So, before we smoke meat and fish, we must brine it! You will use a wet or dry brine depending on what and how you're smoking the food.

Dry brine

Dry brining is commonly used in the production of various cured meats such as ham, bacon, salami and pastrami, as well as fish like salmon and trout. Once cured, rinsed with water to remove excess salt and dried, the meat or fish will develop a pellicle, a sticky surface that gives the smoke something to stick to. It will then be ready to cold smoke over a long period of time. Depending on the type of cured meat or fish, it may require some cooking before serving.

Dry brining or curing is a slower and more subtle technique compared to wet brining. For example, while a fillet of trout might only be cured for around 20 minutes, a large piece of meat might take 48–72 hours. So when curing meat or fish, we need to think about the thickness and adjust the cure time accordingly. Thicker pieces of meat and fish require a longer curing time; while thinner pieces need less time in the brine!

General dry brine for meat
1 measure of table salt to 1 measure of soft brown sugar

For our favourite dry brine recipe when cold smoking pork fillet, lamb loin, duck breast and venison loin for charcuterie, see page 115.

General dry brine for fish
3 measures of table salt to 1 measure of caster sugar

A note about sodium nitrate
Sodium nitrate plays a vital role in the curing process by promoting a chemical change that prevents the growth of harmful pathogens. It also helps meat keep its flavour and colour. Salt (sodium chloride) was used for thousands of years for preservation before refrigeration. A few centuries ago, it was discovered that the presence of nitrates in some salt helped preserve meat for longer. Nitrate also helps to break down tough fats to tenderise the meat.

We have both tried to make bacon with just a salt and sugar brine, but you end up with very salty tasting, grey looking pork. It's not the bacon we know and love! To achieve crispy, smoky, golden-brown bacon, we would recommend you use sodium nitrate. However, it is essential to strike a balance by not relying solely on sodium nitrate, as it can be overpowering. Combining it with salt helps to mitigate its harshness and ensure a more balanced flavour. We recommend a 50:50 ratio of salt to nitrate — just enough for the chemical change.

You can buy sodium nitrate from your butchers or order a home cure saltpetre online. We would both like this not to be the case, but nitrate is the way forward. In many curing and smoking books you will read that it's possible to cure without it, but it isn't, and we want you to be successful with the smoking you try.

Despite its benefits, much has been written about the use of nitrate in curing and the potential for it to react with meat to create carcinogenic properties. Many vegetables, such as celery and spinach, naturally contain high levels of nitrates. The use of nitrate in curing is a much-debated topic worldwide with the Soil Association involved in discussions. Ultimately, the decision to use nitrate in curing is a personal one, and you may want to research further if you have concerns.

From our point of view, it's as simple as this: if you cure pork with just salt and sugar, you will get salty pork; if you use nitrate, you will get bacon!

Wet brine

Wet brining is the process of soaking meat and fish in water, salt and often sugar to retain moisture and enhance flavour and texture. This method is particularly effective for meats that are prone to drying out, such as duck breast, turkey, chicken, beef short ribs, lamb ribs and pork ribs before hot smoking.

While wet brining is suitable for both meat and fish, it's generally accepted that meat responds better than fish. Wet brining fish requires precision and experience to avoid over-brining so we wouldn't recommend it if you're just starting out. Wet brining is generally quicker than dry brining, although both require some forward planning.

For a simple wet brine, use 1 tbsp salt to 1 cup water.

General wet brine recipe
800ml / 3½ cups water
250ml / 1 cup apple juice
80g / ¼ cup salt
70g / ¼ cup maple syrup
2 tbsp soft brown sugar
1 tbsp garlic powder
1 tbsp onion powder

We've suggested our favourite additions to the brine, but there are lots of other flavours you can add, such as treacle or chilli flakes.

For every 500g (1lb) of meat, brine for 1 hour, or halve the time for long, thin cuts, ensuring the meat is fully submerged in the brine.

Brining for hot smoking foods

Hot smoking meat and fish starts with the essential step of brining. Whether you choose wet or dry brining depends on the dish you're preparing. While both meat and fish can be dry brined, meat typically responds better to a wet brine than fish. You will also want to consider the size of the meat and fish to determine the best equipment to use. For example, thin fillets of fish are best dry brined and hot smoked in a covered baking tray on a hob, while larger pieces of meat benefit from a wet brine and a long, slow hot smoke in a barbecue or home hot smoker.

Brining for cold smoking foods

Wet brining before cold smoking is not suitable for beginners! It will break down the tissues in meat and fish and you must really understand the science of what you are doing. So stick to dry brine when you are cold smoking. Hooray!

This is our advice for beginner home smokers. But ultimately, choosing whether to wet or dry brine depends on your desired outcome. However, in this book, we'll recommend which brine to use and whether to hot or cold smoke, so you don't have to figure it out on your own.

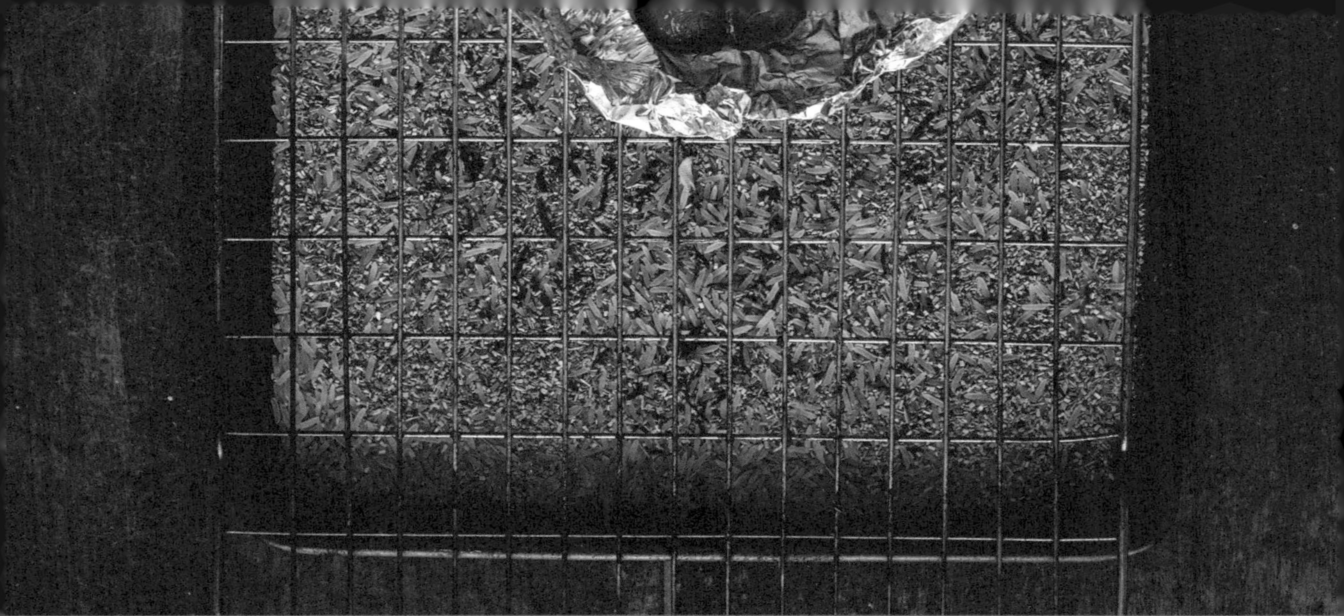

Part one — **Hot smoking**

3
How to
hot smoke
at home

Set up

The easiest way to hot smoke at home is to use the general kit listed on page 17. Place 100g / ½ cup wood dust and 100g / ½ cup rice on a baking tray and position a cooling rack on top. Take your food — we'd suggest starting with one of the vegetables below. Arrange it on the rack and wrap the tray entirely in foil so there are no air gaps. Create a cavity above for smoke to circulate (see photo page 37). Light the gas hob and turn to a low-medium heat for smoking. Be careful not to let the rice and dust burn, as it can make the ingredients taste bitter. For larger vegetables or pieces of meat, you can use a bigger container like a barbecue or home hot smoker.

Vegetables, fruit and dairy

In this section you will find information on the vegetables and dairy items we've used in the hot smoking recipes, but feel free to experiment with other varieties. The times provided are guidelines, so check on progress (by opening the foil) then taste and adjust as you go.

When preparing your vegetables and fruit, each will be cut differently based on its density and moisture content. For example, tomatoes have a high moisture content so need to be sliced thickly to prevent them from drying out during smoking. Remember the hot smoking process both smokes *and* cooks. Some denser vegetables like cauliflower benefit from being blanched before smoking to help them cook faster. To blanch a vegetable, bring a pot of water to the boil and parboil for 3–5 minutes, depending on the size, and drain well. After preparing your vegetables, rub them with olive oil and salt to create a barrier to stop them drying out. The oil will also absorb the smoky flavour.

Potato (white waxy or sweet potato)
Cut into 5mm / ¼in thick slices and smoke for 20 minutes.

Butternut squash
Cut into 5mm / ¼in thick slices and smoke for 20 minutes.

Cauliflower
Cut into 1cm / ½in thick slices, blanch in boiling water for 4 minutes and smoke for 20 minutes.

Broccoli
Cut into florets and smoke for 15 minutes.

Sweetheart cabbage
Cut into 6 lengthways, keeping the core intact and the leaves together. Char for 6 minutes on each side in an oiled pan, then smoke for 20 minutes.

Mushroom
Slice or keep them whole. Smoke for 20–25 minutes.

Cherry tomatoes
Cut in half and place on a little foil 'bowl' to prevent them from falling through the wire rack (photo page 31).

Drizzle with a couple of teaspoons of balsamic vinegar and smoke for 10–15 minutes.

Garlic bulb
Cut in half widthways and smoke for 20 minutes.

Onion
Peel the onion but keep both ends intact to hold it together. Cut it in half lengthways and brush with oil (you can also brush with balsamic vinegar). Smoke for an hour, or longer if you prefer softer onions.

Pineapple
Peel and cut into 1cm / ½in slices and smoke for 20 minutes.

Apple and pear
Quarter and remove the core, then cut into 5mm / ¼in slices and smoke for 15–20 minutes. Works best with ripe pears.

Plums
Cut in half, remove the stones and place the plums in a small foil tray with sugar and balsamic vinegar. Smoke for 20 minutes.

Chocolate
Put the chocolate into a shallow dish. Smoke for 20 minutes until the chocolate is slightly soft.

Cream
Pour the cream into a shallow dish. Smoke for 10 minutes.

Note: Vegetables, fruit, nuts and dairy can be either hot or cold smoked. Because we are not curing the ingredients both processes work. Remember, hot smoking also *cooks* your ingredients, whereas cold smoking purely smokes them.

You can, for instance, hot or cold smoke chocolate or cream (see above). It's worth remembering that the flavour with hot smoking will be a little harsher (it is also being cooked so the smoke strength is stronger). That said, you are more likely to have the equipment you need to hot smoke on the hob or stovetop, rather than a cold smoker. So it's partly taste, partly the smoking equipment you have available, and partly what you want to experiment with.

Meat and fish

Meat and fish must be brined before being smoked. Refer to Chapter 2 on the importance of brining, plus each recipe will tell you whether to wet or dry brine beforehand.

Smoking times are also specified in individual recipes, but below are some recommended smoking times and weights to use as a general guide. As with vegetables and dairy, you can experiment with different woods and smoking times to suit your palate or a specific dish.

Hot smoking times for different meats and fish
Chicken breasts: 1 hour
Chicken wings: 1½ hours
Pork ribs: 5 hours
Lamb ribs: 2½–3 hours
Lamb chops: 1 hour
Venison loin: 1 hour
Duck breasts: 2 hours
Salmon fillet, 200g: 8–10 minutes
Mackerel fillet, 100g: 8 minutes
Haddock, small whole fish: 20 minutes
Haddock fillet: 8–10 minutes
Tiger prawns, skinless: 4–6 minutes

1. Place wood dust and rice on a baking tray and position a cooling rack on top.
2. Arrange the food you are smoking on the rack.
   (NB cabbage shown was chargrilled beforehand)

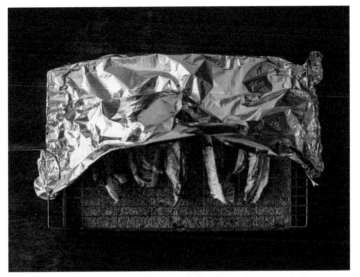

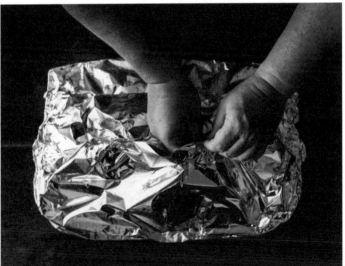

3. Wrap the tray entirely in foil so there are no air gaps.
4. Create a cavity above for smoke to circulate.
   Place baking tray on the hob or stovetop.

4
**Hot smoked
recipes**

Vegetarian

Fish and meat

Desserts

Smoked mushrooms on toast

My entire family have been obsessed with mushrooms ever since I was a little girl. Now, both our children have joined in the fungi love. This recipe is a firm favourite in our house.
— JG

SERVES: *1*
TAKES: *35 minutes (including smoking time)*
KIT: *Hot smoking equipment, wood dust, rice*

125g / 4½oz chestnut mushrooms, sliced
30g / 2 tbsp salted butter (or vegan alternative)
1 garlic clove, finely chopped
45ml / 3 tbsp double cream (or vegan alternative)
1 slice sourdough or your favourite bread, toasted
3 sprigs of parsley, leaves picked off and chopped
salt and black pepper, to taste

Hot smoke the mushrooms for 20–25 minutes (see page 33). Melt the butter in a pan, add the mushrooms and fry for 2–3 minutes until brown, then add the garlic and cook for 30 seconds. Pour in the cream and heat through until warm. Season to taste. Serve on toast, scattered with parsley.

Recipe pictured on page 38–39

Smoked tomato, garlic and olive oil tagliatelle

Tomato sauce with fresh or dried pasta is one of the most popular and easy meals to make at home. This is slightly more complex but takes it to a different level. — JG

SERVES: *2*
TAKES: *30 minutes (including smoking time)*
KIT: *Hot smoking equipment, wood dust, rice*

250g / 9oz cherry tomatoes
4 garlic cloves, thickly sliced
2 tbsp olive oil, plus extra for serving
1 tbsp balsamic vinegar
160g / 5½oz tagliatelle (you can use any pasta here)
grated Parmesan or vegan cheese, to serve
a handful of basil leaves
salt and black pepper, to taste

Cut the tomatoes in half and arrange in foil on your wire rack with the garlic, olive oil and a good glug of balsamic vinegar. Hot smoke for 20 minutes (see page 33).

When you are ready to eat, cook the tagliatelle in boiling salted water until al dente. Drain the pasta and season with salt and pepper, then mix the tomatoes into the pasta. Serve with grated cheese and torn basil leaves.

You can hot smoke other vegetables for this pasta, too.

For smoked butter garlic bread recipe, see page 91

Smoked potato and cheese sourdough pizza with jalapeños and rosemary

I first tried 'pizza bianca' (white pizza, i.e. no tomato sauce) at Testaccio market in Rome with food journalist Rachel Roddy. We ate 'Pizza con Patate' and I've loved playing around with potato pizza ever since. — JG

MAKES: *4*
TAKES: *2 days (including making the sourdough)*
KIT: *Hot and cold smoking equipment, wood dust, rice*
—

For the thin crust pizza dough
240g / 2 cups plain flour, plus extra for dusting
240g / 2 cups strong flour
7g / ¼oz fast action yeast
8g / ¼oz salt
140g / 5oz sourdough starter
240ml / 1 cup warm water
2 tsp olive oil
semolina, for dusting

For the topping
600g / 1lb 5oz potato, peeled and thinly sliced
360g / 12oz cheese (cheddar is good)
8 tsp chopped jalapeños
8 tsp capers
4 garlic cloves, finely chopped
4 tsp chopped rosemary
olive oil
100g / 3½oz rocket

(continued overleaf)

For the pizza dough, combine all the dry ingredients with the sourdough starter in a large bowl, then slowly mix in water until you have a smooth, dough-like consistency — you may not need it all.

Add the oil and mix again. Let it prove for 2 hours, then gently knock back the dough, cover and leave it overnight at room temperature.

The next day, knead the dough briefly and then divide it into 4 balls and place on a floured baking tray. Place in a bag or cover with foil and refrigerate overnight. Remove from the fridge a couple of hours before use.

Cold smoke the cheddar for 4 hours (see page 82), then grate it. Hot smoke the potato slices (see page 33) but just for 10 minutes as the potato doesn't need to be cooked all the way through.

Preheat the oven to its highest setting, usually 240°C (475°F), and use baking/pizza stone. If you don't have one, build the pizza on a baking tray and place in the oven when ready.

Sprinkle semolina on a baking tray. Roll out a dough ball to approx. 5cm / 2in each and place on baking tray. Arrange the potatoes to cover the pizza bases, leaving a 2cm / ¾in border around the edge. Top with the cheese, jalapeños, capers, garlic and rosemary, then drizzle with olive oil and season with salt and pepper. With care, slide the pizza from the baking tray onto the hot baking/pizza stone in the oven (or simply place baking tray into the oven). Bake for 6–10 minutes until golden and brown around the edges (timing depends on how hot your oven gets). Slice and top each with a handful of rocket.

Smoked vegetable spanakopita with smoked cashew cheese

Always a favourite vegetarian centrepiece when I'm catering, or hosting my sister Meriel's family. Over the years, I've adapted it to become a fabulous vegan choice; smoking some of the ingredients takes it to another level. You can, of course, substitute eggs and smoked feta for flax and cashew cheese. Any smoked vegetable is delicious here. — JG

SERVES: *4–6*
TAKES: *3 hours 30 minutes (including smoking time)*
KIT: *Hot and cold smoking equipment, wood dust, rice*
—

olive oil
1 medium red or white onion, roughly chopped
500g / 1lb 2oz spinach
a large bunch of dill, finely chopped
50g / ¼ cup currants, soaked in hot water for 15 minutes and drained
50g / ½ cup capers
3 flax eggs (3 tbsp ground flaxseed mixed with 3 tbsp water and left for 5 minutes)
100g / 3½oz sundried tomatoes, chopped
8 sheets filo pastry
150g / 5oz hot smoked potato slices (see page 33)
250g / 9oz hot smoked broccoli or cauliflower florets (see page 33)
1 portion cashew cheese (see below)
1 tbsp sesame seeds (black or white)

(continued overleaf)

For the smoked cashew cheese

150g / 1 cup cashews, soaked in water overnight
6 tsp nutritional yeast
juice of 1–2 lemons
2 tsp olive oil
1 hot or cold smoked garlic clove, grated (optional and to taste)
salt and black pepper, to taste

First make the cashew cheese. Drain the cashews, pat them dry with kitchen paper and then coat in olive oil and cold smoke for 2 hours. Blitz the cold smoked cashews, nutritional yeast, lemon juice, olive oil and garlic (if using) in a blender and season to taste with salt and pepper. This cashew cheese keeps for 3 days in an airtight container in fridge. You can also freeze it without any problems.

To make the spanakopita, preheat the oven to 180°C (350°F). Heat a little oil in a large frying pan and gently fry the onion for 10 minutes until softened. Tip into a large bowl, then add the spinach to the same pan and sauté until wilted. Tip into a sieve and squeeze out any excess moisture, then add to the onion in the bowl. Add the dill, currants, capers, flax eggs and sundried tomatoes, then season with salt and pepper.

Place the filo on a board and cover with a slightly damp tea towel to stop it from drying out. Next, oil a small, deep baking dish (20 × 15cm / 8 × 6in or a round one if that's what you have) and start layering in the pastry. Brush oil onto the first layer of pastry, then lay it over the base and over one side of dish. Repeat this process, alternating sides each time until the base and all sides of the dish are covered.

Spread the prepared spinach mixture evenly in the dish, then add dollops of cashew cheese. Finally layer with the potatoes and broccoli or cauliflower. Once the dish is filled, fold the layers of pastry over the top, tucking in any extra bits.

Lightly oil the top of the pastry and scatter over the sesame seeds. Place the dish in the oven and bake for 40 minutes, or until the pastry turns golden brown. Delicious served with a green salad and some kraut.

For smoked houmous recipe, see page 101

Smoked trout with fennel, blood orange and rocket salad

This was the first recipe I smoked. Scott taught me while we were both working at Llys Meddyg, a hotel and restaurant in Newport, Wales. I'd never done anything like it before and it was so simple I couldn't believe it. I've made it many times since then. If you've never smoked anything before, this is a brilliant place to start.— JG

SERVES: *2*
TAKES: *1 hour 10 minutes (including smoking time)*
KIT: *Hot smoking equipment, Lapsang Souchong, wood dust, rice*

———

2 trout fillets
100g / 3½oz rocket
1 bulb of fennel, thinly sliced or shaved with a peeler, fronds reserved
1 blood orange or juicy regular orange
freshly ground black pepper
flaky sea salt
extra virgin olive oil

For the dry brine
½ tsp flaked salt
½ tsp soft brown muscovado sugar

Dry brine the trout for 1 hour (see page 25).

While the trout is brining, set up your hot smoker (see page 32 if using hob method). Smoke the trout for 8–10 minutes, then allow it to cool.

Meanwhile, assemble the salad on a platter. Start with the rocket, then layer the thinly sliced fennel on top. Remove all the peel and pith from the orange with a sharp knife, then cut into thin horizontal slices and add these to the salad.

Once cooled, flake the smoked trout over the salad. Finish with fennel fronds, freshly ground black pepper, flaky sea salt and a drizzle of olive oil.

Smoked salmon blinis with crème fraîche and dill

Salmon is often the first thing that comes to mind when we think of smoked foods. It's a food we associate with celebrations — always a winner at a party, as a starter on Christmas day or a weekend treat. Its rich, salty and smoky flavour makes it a versatile ingredient that can be enjoyed in many different forms — as a standalone appetiser, incorporated into salads or used as a topping for canapés. I first learnt to hot smoke salmon with Scott and it's always stuck with me how something I once thought so complex can be so simple. — JG

MAKES: *36 small blinis*
TAKES: *2 hours (including smoking time)*
KIT: *Hot smoking equipment, wood dust, rice*
—

3 skin-on salmon fillets, approx. 200g / 7oz each
250g / 1 cup crème fraîche
a small bunch of dill
capers (optional)
freshly ground black pepper

For the dry brine
½ tsp flaked salt
½ tsp soft brown muscovado sugar

For the blinis
110g / 1 cup plain flour
½ tsp cream of tartar
¼ tsp bicarbonate of soda
2 tsp caster sugar
a pinch of salt

(continued overleaf)

1 small egg
140ml / ⅔ cup whole milk
salted butter, for frying

To cure and smoke the salmon, first dry brine the salmon fillets for 1 hour, then hot smoke on a covered baking tray for 8–10 minutes. After removing from the heat, leave the salmon covered with the foil until cool. Flake the fish and put to one side.

While the salmon is brining, prepare the blinis: mix all the dry ingredients together, then add the egg, and whisk in the milk. Leave the mixture to stand for 30 minutes.

Place a frying pan over a medium heat and add a knob of butter; when melted drop in 2 teaspoons of batter for each blini. Cook on each side for 1–2 minutes, or until golden brown. You will see bubbles forming inside the blini; this shows it's cooked through. Continue until all the batter is used up.

Once the blinis have cooled, add a teaspoon of crème fraîche to each one (sour cream is also good here) and some dill. Adorn with your flaked smoky fish, then add capers (if using) and a grind of black pepper to finish.

Smoky prawn and butternut laksa

When I worked at Providores in London, we always had a laksa on the menu. This creamy, sweet and spicy noodle soup is made with a coconut-milk-based broth flavoured with spices such as lemongrass or galangal. What sets this dish apart is the smoky flavour infused into the soup by smoking the fish bones beforehand. It's a simple step that transforms the dish. Looking back at my career, there are certain recipes that stay with me: this laska is one of them. — SD

SERVES: *6*

TAKES: *1 hour 15 minutes (including smoking time)*

KIT: *Hot smoking equipment, jasmine tea, rice*

NOTE: *If you want to simplify the dish and avoid handling fish heads, you can smoke the prawns instead. Hot smoke them in the same way for 5–6 minutes and add them to the laksa at the end.*

———

500g / 1lb 2oz flat fish bones/heads
1.5 litres / 6 cups chicken stock
300g / 11oz butternut squash skin on, cut in 3cm / 1in wedges
200g / 7oz dried egg or rice noodles
5 tbsp sesame oil
24 raw tiger prawns, cleaned and washed
2 hot green chillies, thinly sliced
6 lime leaves (fresh or dried)
12 thin slices of galangal (or ginger)
6 garlic cloves, thinly sliced
1 small white onion, diced
2 tsp light soy sauce
2 tbsp tamarind paste
400ml / 14fl oz can unsweetened coconut milk
3 tbsp or juice of 2 limes

(continued overleaf)

2 tsp Thai fish sauce
sliced red chilli
a bunch of coriander, leaves picked
150g / 5oz beansprouts

Prepare your hot smoker with jasmine tea and rice, then hot smoke the fish bones/heads, eyes and gills removed, for 30 minutes and set aside.

In a large pot, bring the chicken stock to the boil. Add the smoked fish bones/heads and simmer for 20 minutes, then carefully remove them from the stock and discard. Add the butternut squash to the pot and simmer until cooked, about 10 minutes, then remove from the pot and keep it warm.

Cook the noodles in the stock according to the packet instructions. Drain them through a sieve into a large saucepan, keeping the stock.

Return the empty pot to a high heat and heat 2 tablespoons of the sesame oil until hot. Add the prawns and fry for 2 minutes. Set them aside with the butternut squash.

Add the remaining sesame oil to the pot; once hot, add the green chillies, lime leaves, galangal, garlic and onion. Fry for 1 minute over a high heat, stirring throughout. Pour in the smoked fish stock, soy sauce, tamarind paste and coconut milk. Simmer for 5 minutes, then add the lime juice. Season with fish sauce to taste.

Divide the noodles, butternut squash and prawns into 6 bowls, then ladle the hot broth over the top. Garnish each serving with sliced red chilli, coriander leaves and beansprouts.

Smoked duck with pickled cherries

I'm always thinking about balancing flavours and textures.
In this recipe, the richness of the duck is beautifully balanced
with the tanginess of the pickled cherries, the aromatic notes
of cardamom and the crunchy texture of the pistachio.
The smoky flavours just take it to another level. — SD

SERVES: *2*

TAKES: *2 days (including brining and smoking time)*

KIT: *Hot smoking equipment, oak shavings*

For the wet brine (for 1.5kg / 3lb duck breast meat)

750ml / 3 cups warm tap water
225g / 1 cup soft light brown sugar
175g / ½ cup black treacle
112g / 4oz table salt
112g / 4oz sodium nitrate

For the sweet and sour pickled cherries

100g / ¾ cup dried cherries
100g / ½ cup caster sugar
100ml / scant ½ cup red wine vinegar
1 star anise
½ cinnamon stick

For the cheddar cheese dressing

2 tbsp lemon juice or white wine vinegar
2 tsp minced garlic
¼ tsp Dijon mustard
125g / ½ cup sour cream
2 tbsp mayonnaise
110g / 3½oz vintage cheddar, half grated / half crumbled
salt and black pepper, to taste

(continued overleaf)

For the smoked duck salad
1 hot smoked duck breast
2 large handfuls of rocket
1 whole head of chicory, leaves separated
1 tbsp chopped pistachios

Start by mixing all the brine ingredients together. We're using a 50 per cent nitrate/salt blend (see page 26) and we're also using treacle in the brine, which gives the meat a liquoricy depth of flavour. Submerge the duck in the brine and refrigerate for at least 12 hours or overnight. Remove the duck from the brine and place it back in the fridge but this time uncovered for an additional day to air dry.

Prepare your smoker with oak shavings. The bold flavours of the oak pairs well with the richness of the duck. Set the smoker to 90–100°C (194–212°F) and smoke the duck breast for 2 hours until it reaches an internal temperature of 45–50°C (113–122°F). Once done, let the duck breast rest for a few minutes before slicing.

For the pickled cherries, combine all ingredients except the cherries in a pan and heat until the sugar dissolves. Pour the mixture over the cherries in a heatproof bowl and set aside for 24 hours. They can be stored in the fridge up to 3 weeks.

To prepare the cheddar dressing, mix the lemon juice, garlic and mustard together. Slowly whisk in the cheese until it binds, then add the sour cream and mayonnaise. Lastly, add the grated cheddar and season to taste.

To assemble the dish, place chicory leaves and a scattering of rocket over 2 plates. Add thinly sliced smoked duck breast, then top with the pickled cherries and a drizzle of cheddar dressing. Sprinkle over the crumbled cheddar and pistachios.

Smoked lamb ribs with gochujang ketchup and rosemary labneh

I love ribs! I love lamb! And I for sure love the flavour of lamb fat! I tend to gravitate towards Asian flavours and then get pulled back to my Welsh roots. In this dish, we have a bit of both going on with lamb, rosemary and Korean chilli. Oh, and let's not forget that beautiful smoky flavour. — SD

SERVES: *4*
TAKES: *4 hours (including brining and smoking time)*
KIT: *Hot smoking equipment, hickory, maple or oak shavings*
—

For the lamb
8 lamb ribs
large handful of coriander
1 tbsp toasted sesame seeds

For the rosemary labneh
125g / ½ cup Greek yoghurt
2 tbsp olive oil
1 tsp finely chopped rosemary
1 tsp finely chopped tarragon
zest and juice of ½ lemon
salt and black pepper, to taste

For the gochujang ketchup
120g / 4oz gochujang
4 tbsp rice wine vinegar
150g / 5oz tahini
80ml / ⅓ cup sesame oil
3 tbsp soy sauce
90g / ½ cup caster sugar
55g / 2oz roast garlic, minced

(continued overleaf)

Prepare the lamb first, as this will take around 1 hour in a wet brine depending on weight (1 hour brine per 500g / 1lb 2oz meat). Refer to page 28 for the wet brine recipe. Hot smoke the brined lamb ribs for 2½–3 hours.

Meanwhile, prepare the labneh. Strain the yoghurt through a muslin suspended over a bowl for 3 hours. Mix the strained yoghurt with all the remaining ingredients (keep the whey for other uses, like scones). Leave for about 1 hour before serving.

Prepare the ketchup by combining all the ingredients in a bowl and mixing well. Allow it to sit for about 1 hour and it's ready to go.

Once you've smoked the lamb ribs, liberally brush them with the ketchup. Return the ribs to the smoker or barbecue and cook for 5 minutes, or until heated through and sticky.

Place the lamb ribs on a plate and serve with the rosemary labneh. Garnish with coriander leaves and toasted sesame seeds.

Smoked Thai BBQ chicken wings

These succulent chicken wings are inspired by my time working with Jean-Georges Vongerichten in New York. They're everything you'd want from a chicken wing and more: sticky, sweet, spicy and smoky. Best served with a cold beer. — SD

SERVES: *4*
TAKES: *3 hours 30 minutes*
(including brining and smoking time)
KIT: *Hot smoking equipment and hickory or maple shavings*

---

16 chicken wings (approx. 1kg / 2lb 4oz)
100g / 1 cup chopped toasted peanuts
2 red chillies, sliced
6 spring onions, sliced
a bunch of coriander, leaves picked

For the marinade
4 tbsp vegetable oil
50g / ½ cup thinly sliced shallots
30g / ¼ cup thinly sliced garlic
1 tbsp dried chilli flakes
½ fresh red Thai chilli
30g / 1oz piece of galangal (or ginger)
    cut into 5mm / ¼in slices
⅛ tsp Thai shrimp paste
2 tbsp soft dark brown sugar
2 tbsp tamarind paste
2 tbsp red wine vinegar
2 tbsp lime juice
¾ tsp Thai fish sauce
¾ tsp salt

(continued overleaf)

Prepare the chicken wings first, as they will take around 2 hours in a wet brine (see page 28) depending on the weight (1 hour brine per 500g / 1lb 2oz meat). Once brined, hot smoke the chicken wings for 1 hour at 90°C (194°F).

Prepare the marinade while the chicken wings are smoking. Heat the oil in a medium pan and fry the shallots and garlic over a medium heat until golden. Add the remaining ingredients to the pan and bring to the boil, then reduce the heat and simmer for 1 minute.

Transfer the mixture to a blender and blitz until smooth, taking care when blending hot ingredients. Set the sauce aside in a container.

When the chicken wings have been hot smoked for 1 hour, remove them from the smoker and coat them in the marinade. Return the wings to the smoker for another 30 minutes at the same temperature until they are sticky.

Garnish with the peanuts, chilli, spring onion and coriander leaves. Serve and enjoy!

Smoked beef brisket (pastrami)

I first discovered my love of brisket from my Gran's boiled dinners. She would boil a large piece of brined beef brisket with vegetables in a large pot. We'd all gather round the table and argue over who got the last slice. After that, during my two-year stint working with Jean-Georges Vongerichten in New York and upstate at Lake Placid Lodge, I developed an obsession with salt beef and pastrami — which is essentially smoked brisket; it's much more common in America than west Wales! I would quite often serve salt beef for staff dinners with the restaurant's leftover dauphinoise potatoes. A salty, creamy match made in heaven. — SD

SERVES: *6*
TAKES: *10 days for brining + 6 hours smoking time*
KIT: *Hot smoker or barbecue, oak shavings*
—

1kg / 2lb 4oz beef brisket

For the beef brine (based on brining 1kg / 2lb 4oz beef)
1 garlic clove
4 tsp caster sugar
1 tsp allspice
1 tsp mustard powder
1 tsp ground cloves
1 tsp ground coriander
½ cinnamon stick
½ tsp cinnamon powder
30g / 1oz shallot, finely chopped
1 bay leaf
125g / 1 cup salt
25g / 1oz sodium nitrate
1.4 litres / 6 cups water

For the dry rub

4 tbsp black peppercorns

4 tbsp coriander seeds

1 tbsp smoked paprika

2 tsp garlic powder

2 tsp onion powder

1 tsp yellow mustard seeds

4 tbsp soft light brown sugar

2 tbsp American mustard

First make the brine. Put all the ingredients in a large saucepan and bring to a simmer. Heat through gently, until the sugar and salt have dissolved completely; this should take about 10 minutes. Pour the brine into a plastic container with a lid and put in the fridge until completely cold.

Prepare the beef for brining by trimming off any excess fat and sinew. If the meat is thicker than 2.5cm / 1in, you'll need to make cuts into the joint (with the grain) deep enough to see the middle of the joint. This is so that the brine will penetrate the centre of the meat. Place the joint in a container or ziplock bag and cover with brine — just enough to cover the meat. Top up with a little extra cold water if needed and seal the container completely. Leave in the fridge for 10 days and rotate every day.

After this time, remove the brisket from the brine and wash well under cold water. Pat dry with kitchen paper, then leave to come to room temperature.

To make the dry rub, grind up all the rub spices along with the sugar using a pestle and mortar or in the small bowl of a food processor. Apply a thin layer of American mustard all over the meat. Then rub spice mix over all sides of the meat.

(continued overleaf)

Place the beef in the hot smoker (you will need to use a hot smoker or barbecue for larger pieces of meat, rather than on the hob) and smoke for about 6 hours at 110°C (230°F) until the internal meat temperature hits 70°C (158°F). It's a nice balance between getting the smoky flavour and getting the meat cooked and over the line. Use your meat thermometer to check it is properly cooked.

Pastrami Reuben sandwich

I love this sandwich. Traditionally, the Reuben is made of thinly sliced corned beef, Swiss cheese and sauerkraut on rye bread slathered with Russian dressing — but I'm using our delicious smoked pastrami here. You can't go wrong with either, just be sure to be liberal with the meat. Reuben sandwiches are on the menu of every other deli in New York. When I lived there, I would find it almost impossible to not order this sandwich whenever I walked past my local. — SD

SERVES: *2*

TAKES: *30 minutes*

KIT: *Hot smoker or barbecue, oak shavings*

——

300g / 10½oz homemade pastrami (see page 66)
4 slices light rye bread
4 slices Swiss cheese, e.g. Emmental
butter, for spreading
sauerkraut
dill pickles / gherkins

(continued overleaf)

For the Russian dressing

1 tbsp onion, finely diced

1 tbsp dill pickle / gherkin, finely diced

170g / ¾ cup mayonnaise

60g / ¼ cup sour cream (or use more mayo)

2½ tbsp sriracha, spicy ketchup or chilli sauce
(or use 4 tbsp ketchup + 2 tsp Tabasco)

3 tsp horseradish sauce, or to taste

1 tsp Worcestershire sauce

¼ tsp sweet paprika

Make the Russian dressing by mixing together all the ingredients until combined. Chill in the fridge for at least 20 minutes. The dressing will keep for up to 2 weeks in the fridge.

Thinly slice the pastrami. If it has just come out of the smoker and it's hot, there's never a better time to eat it. But if not, you can reheat on a griddle or in a microwave.

Place a frying pan or a griddle over a medium heat. To assemble a sandwich, take 2 slices of bread. Butter one side of each slice (this becomes the *outsides* of your sandwich when it's griddled), and spread a teaspoon of dressing on the other side. Place the warm pastrami on top of the dressing, add 2 tablespoons of sauerkraut, then your cheese. Top with the second slice, and press down. So the outsides of your sandwich should be buttered.

Place the sandwich in the hot frying pan or griddle. Slowly brown the sandwich on each side until crispy and warm through.

Cut in half, and serve with dill pickles or gherkins.

Smoked chocolate mousse

When I was in New York, I hosted corporate retreats at a place called Lake Placid Lodge. While the city workers spent the day skiing, I'd get the barbecue ready to make hot chocolate for their return. One day, we accidentally burnt the chocolate. We kind of liked it, but we knew it needed refining. So that's when we worked on a smoked hot chocolate, which we developed into this rich, creamy, but delicate chocolate mousse. — SD

SERVES: *4*
TAKES: *3 hours (including smoking time)*
KIT: *Hot smoking equipment, oak chips, rice*

175g / 6oz dark chocolate (at least 55% cocoa solids)
2 eggs
60g / ¼ cup muscovado sugar
60g / 4 tbsp unsalted butter
a pinch of salt
240ml / 1 cup double cream
2 tsp almond extract
caster sugar, to taste
raspberries or cherries, to serve

Put the chocolate into a shallow tray and smoke it on your hob for around 20 minutes (see page 34). Don't smoke it too hard — we only do this until the chocolate is slightly soft and the smoke sticks to the fat in the chocolate.

Separate the egg whites from the yolks. Whisk the egg whites to a stiff peak.

Bring a saucepan of water to the boil and place a stainless-steel bowl over the top. Add the muscovado sugar, butter and salt to the bowl and stir until everything is combined.

Remove from the heat. Stir in the melted chocolate, followed by the egg yolks until smooth, then carefully fold in the egg whites. Divide the mousse into 4 glass jars or bowls and chill in the fridge for a good few hours.

Whisk together the double cream and almond extract until stiff and add some caster sugar to taste. Serve the mousse with a dollop of the whipped cream and maybe a few raspberries or cherries.

Smoked ice cream

Hot smoked ice cream was another unexpected discovery during my time experimenting with flavours at Lake Placid Lodge in New York. After accidentally burning hot chocolate, we discovered that chocolate absorbed smoke beautifully, inspiring us to explore its potential with cream. A valuable lesson learned from this process: fat is a *vehicle* for smoke! The result? Smoky, creamy, velvety soft ice cream — a real stand out dish at any dinner party. For this recipe, I use an ice cream maker. — SD

SERVES: *6*
TAKES: *24 hours (including smoking and freezing time)*
KIT: *Hot smoking equipment, rice, hickory shavings*

———

600ml / 2½ cups double cream
2 tbsp whole milk
250g / 1¼ cups caster sugar
a pinch of salt
1 tsp vanilla paste

In a bowl, whisk together all of the ingredients until combined then pour the mixture into a shallow tray. Smoke on the hob for approximately 10 minutes; the mixture should develop a subtle yellow hue and delicate smoky flavour.

Chill the smoked mixture in the fridge overnight, or for several hours until cold. Once chilled, churn the mixture in an ice cream maker until thick and creamy. Transfer to an airtight, freezer proof container and freeze until firm.

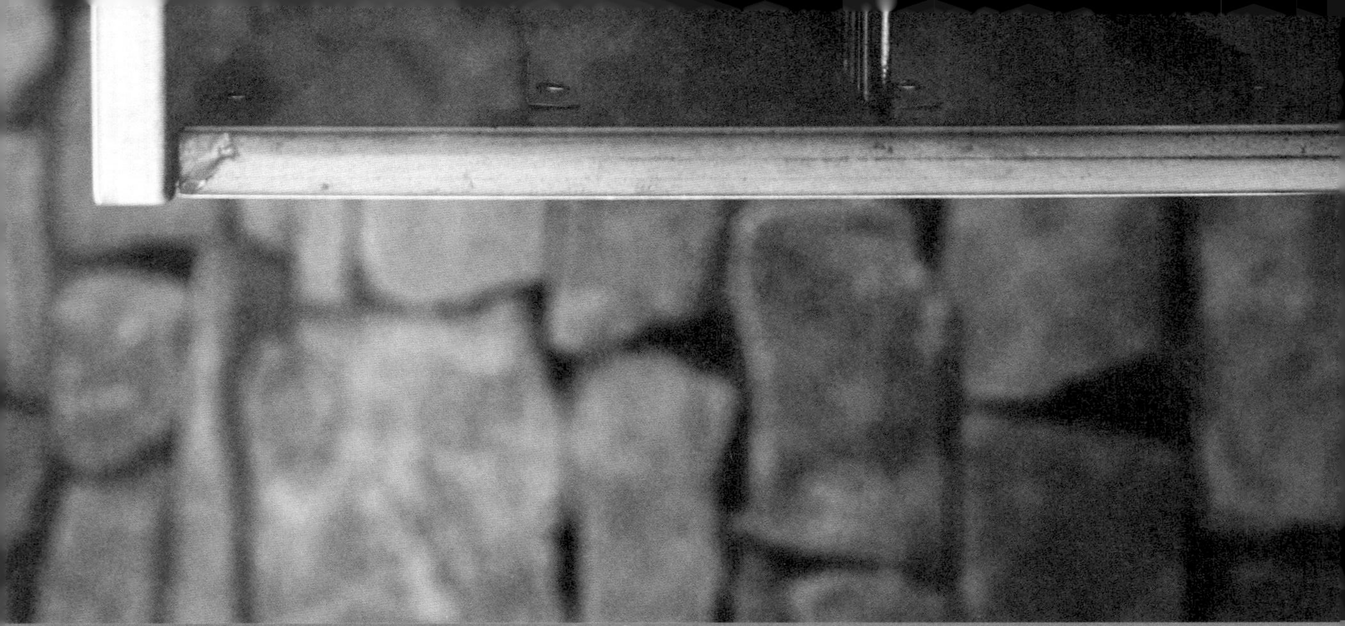

Part two — **Cold smoking**

5
How to
cold smoke
at home

The simplest way to cold smoke at home is to use a smoke generator coil (pictured on page 19) placed in the bottom of your cold smoker. We both use the simple ProQ smoker and it does the job. If you want to have a go at making your own temporary cold smoker, you'll find instructions on how to make one using a cardboard box on page 85.

Fill the smoke generator coil with wood dust or chips, and light the candle/fuel. The wood will smoulder and produce smoke. It's important to keep an eye on the generator to ensure it continues to smoulder and maintains a temperature below 25°C (77°F). Monitoring your smoker is like meditation. You will need to be present and adjust the smoker according to the outside wind direction to ensure you have a good draught. You will also need to refill the smoke generator coil periodically with wood dust or chips. Take a little time to get to know your smoker.

A few notes

Be mindful of sunlight: If you use your smoker in direct sunlight, the temperature will be higher so it's best to move it into shade.

Outside temperature is key: In summer, when outside temperatures reach 30°c (86°f), it's hard to maintain a low smoking temperature. Opt to smoke during cooler times, such as at night or early in the morning, and always smoke under 25°c (77°f), otherwise things start to cook. If it's cold outside you might have to smoke for longer.

Flavour develops over time: We find everything tastes better the day after smoking.

Understand the process: The brine or cure primarily 'cooks' the meat or fish, while the smoking is for preservation, texture and flavour.

Cold smoking essentials: For dairy, nuts, fruit and vegetables we don't need to cure as we are looking at adding new flavours rather than cooking. We recommend lightly coating some vegetables in oil to enhance smoke absorption (see below). If you are lighting up your smoker it's worth filling every shelf. You could do one tray of chickpeas, another with cheese and another with any vegetables you find in your fridge.

Vegetables, fruit and nuts

Preparation

Preparing your fruit, vegetables, nuts and pulses before cold smoking is essential to ensure optimal flavour and texture. Each ingredient may require different preparation methods to ensure the desired outcome.

For example, vegetables like carrots benefit from shaving with a peeler to create long thin strips and blanching in boiling water before being coated in olive oil, while mushrooms simply need slicing and coating in oil.

Nuts, such as cashews, can be smoked straight after being coated in oil, or for a creamier texture, soaked overnight before smoking. Chickpeas and other cooked pulses are delicious when lightly coated in oil.

Once you've prepared your fruit, vegetables, nuts or pulses, arrange them on trays in the cold smoker, ensuring they are spread out evenly to allow for proper smoke circulation. Smoke these ingredients over apple wood dust or similar.

The fruit, vegetables, nuts and pulses below are all used in the recipes that follow. Try experimenting with different varieties and smoking times to achieve a flavour profile that suits your taste.

Carrots
Shave with a peeler to create long thin strips, then blanch in boiling water for 2½ minutes. Cool, and dry on a tea towel. Lightly coat in olive oil and smoke for 2 hours, then add a little salt and lemon juice. Tastes like a vegan smoked salmon.

Beetroot
Peel then boil until tender (around 45 minutes–1 hour), then chop into 2cm / ¾ in chunks and smoke for 30 minutes.

Mushrooms
Slice and lightly coat in olive oil then smoke for 2 hours. Delicious as they are with some salt, in a salad, or fried on toast.

Sweetheart cabbage
Cut into 6 lengthways, keeping the core intact and the leaves together. Char for 5 minutes on each side in an oiled frying pan (or griddle pan if you have one), then lightly coat with olive oil and smoke for 2 hours.

Corn cob (or canned sweetcorn)
For corn cobs, cook them first and smoke for 35–45 minutes. For canned sweetcorn, dry on a tea towel, lightly coat in olive oil and smoke for 2 hours. Lovely in a salad or on a pizza.

Garlic
Peel and smoke whole cloves for 2 hours.

Pineapple
Peel and slice thickly then smoke for 2 hours.

Chickpeas (or other pulses)
If using canned chickpeas, drain, rinse and pat dry with kitchen paper. Spread out on a tray with a light coating of olive oil and smoke for 2 hours.

Cashews
Lightly coat in olive oil and smoke for 2 hours. For a creamier texture, soak cashews overnight before smoking. You can also try smoking sunflower seeds or sesame seeds for 1 hour.

Fresh chillies
These require a longer smoking time (24 hours). Consider adding them to the cold smoker when smoking meat or fish. It's good to dry them out a little beforehand, too. You can also dehydrate in a dehydrator or air fryer afterwards to create a powder similar to paprika.

Additional tips
You can smoke condiments like chutney or tomato sauce by spreading them out on a tray and smoking for 1 hour. You can also cold smoke oils — try vegetable, olive or rapeseed — to enhance the flavour in any recipe. Pour as much as you need into a ceramic or metal dish and smoke for 2 hours.

Dairy, eggs and vegan alternatives

Cold smoking dairy, eggs and vegan alternatives is so much fun — you can literally smoke anything! Dairy products like cheese, butter, milk and cream, as well as many vegan alternatives, often have a high fat content, which acts as a sponge to the smoky flavour. These ingredients also have robust textures that can withstand the smoking process without compromising their structure. Many dairy products and vegan alternatives have relatively neutral flavours, so the smoke adds depth and can complement a range of dishes, from savoury to sweet.

Here are some tips to get you started:

— **Smoke source:** Use apple wood dust or a similar wood for smoking.

— **Preparation:** Fill up the whole smoker with a range of ingredients at the same time.

— **Temperature:** Bring dairy products like butter, cheese and milk or cream to room temperature before smoking.

— **Equipment:** Place ingredients in a metal or ceramic dish (not glass or plastic) to smoke.

Now, let's break down the smoking times and preparation methods for the dairy ingredients and vegan alternatives we have used in the recipes.

Cheese

You can smoke any hard cheese — start with a simple cheddar and see how you like it and then experiment with other varieties, e.g. feta. Place the block on a tray and smoke for 4 hours (it's quicker if you chop it up). Try as you go to get your desired smoky flavour. Smoking enhances a regular cheddar into something special — it's fabulous on toast, pizza, soups or in cauliflower cheese.

Vegan cheese
Smoke whole or in slices on a tray for 4 hours. Some of the oils will come out, but you can still slice and use it as usual.

Butter
Add the butter to a shallow dish or tray and smoke for 2 hours.

Milk
Pour the milk into a shallow dish or container and smoke for 2 hours.

Cream
Pour the cream (single or double cream) into a shallow dish or container and smoke for 2 hours. You can use this to make a deliciously smoky panna cotta (see page 130).

Dark chocolate
Place the bar whole or broken up into pieces onto a tray and smoke for 2 hours. Breaking up the chocolate into pieces increases the surface area for smoking — they should stay whole. If they melt slightly, they will solidify on cooling and be easy to remove.

Hard-boiled eggs
Hard-boil the eggs for 10 minutes, peel then smoke for 2 hours. Perfect for salads, snacking or on buttered toast.

Oat milk
Pour the oat milk into a shallow dish or container and smoke for 2 hours.

Tofu
Chop into smaller pieces for better smoking results. Place on a tray and smoke for 3 hours.

Meat and fish

Preparation

Preparing meat and fish for cold smoking requires careful attention to detail and patience to achieve the best flavour and texture. Each type of protein, whether it's salmon, tuna, pork belly for bacon, or even shellfish, needs a different technique to ensure the best results. For example, curing salmon in a citrus-infused dry brine before smoking adds a delicate tanginess, while curing pork with maple and juniper dry brine creates a sweet and smoky flavour profile.

Understanding the role of ingredients like sodium nitrate (see page 26) in the curing process is essential for food safety and preservation. With a bit of preparation, the right ingredients — and guidance! — you can elevate ordinary cuts of meat and fish to extraordinary culinary creations. So long as you get the science of dry brining right (see pages 25–26), you can experiment with different flavours to suit your taste.

Before smoking, wash off the brine mixture and leave your meat or fish in the fridge uncovered overnight to make sure the flesh is dry and sticky. Do not put wet meat into cold smoke.

Cold smoking times for different meats and fish

Venison loin: 12 hours
Duck breasts: 12 hours
Pork loin: 12 hours
Lamb loin: 12 hours
Salmon, side of: 11–16 hours
Haddock fillet: 8–10 hours

Note these timings can be adjusted depending on the depth of smokiness you prefer. Feel free to experiment!

How to make a cardboard box cold smoker
By Dan Gritten

I've been smoking (mostly salmon) for around 12 years now and have built myself a plywood smoker, but started by using a cardboard box. Here are some simple (I hope) instructions for making your own.

You will need:
1 large cardboard box, say 60cm/24in (L) × 40cm/15in (W) × 50cm/20in (H)
1 smoke generator (such as the ProQ)
7–10 2m/79in bamboo canes
Ceramic tile or metal tray (big enough for the generator to sit on)
Duct tape or parcel tape
A tape measure
A pencil
Secateurs
Smoking wood dust
Tea light

Method
Place the box on a surface smallest end down so that the opening sides are vertical. Tape along one long seam to create the back. The opening flaps are the front (image 1).

Take your pencil and mark two horizontal lines on the sides of the box — one halfway up and one three-quarters of the way up. Starting at the front, mark along these lines at 5cm/2in intervals (image 2).

Using the pencil, make holes through the box at the 5cm/2in marks along each line.

Push the bamboo canes through the holes on one side and out the corresponding hole opposite. Cut the cane with secateurs so about 5cm/2in protrudes on each side. You should now have two racks (image 3).

Place the tile or metal tray in the bottom of the box and move the box outside, placing it onto a non-flammable surface.

Place your prepared ingredients on the racks.

Fill the generator with your preferred wood dust and light according to its instructions. Place the generator on the tile or tray in the bottom of the box.

Close the box flaps and tape closed with a few small pieces of tape. You don't need to achieve a completely airtight seal.

Leave until the generator has stopped smoking — or however long the recipe instructs.

Enjoy!

Notes

Depending on the size of your box and the ingredients you intend to smoke, you can change the spacing of the canes to suit your needs or even make a third rack.

You can place a metal tray on the lower rack to prevent anything dropping onto the generator.

If it looks like it's going to rain when you're using your cardboard smoker, be sure to cover it with a tarpaulin or polythene sheet.

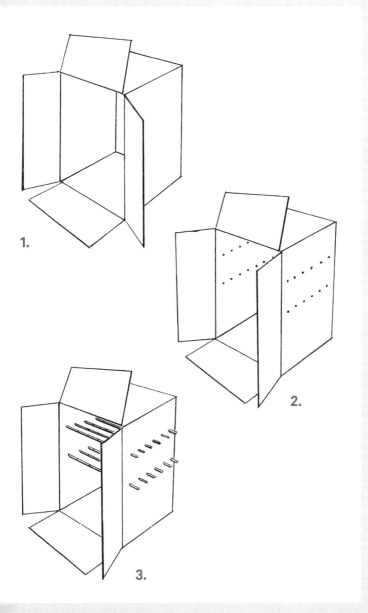

1.

2.

3.

Vegetarian

Fish and meat

Desserts

Smoked butter garlic bread

What's not to love about garlic bread? It's the gateway to garlic and is always a crowd-pleaser with a lasagne or your favourite pasta dish, or as a nibble at a party. — JG

SERVES: *6*
TAKES: *2 hours 30 minutes (including smoking time)*
KIT: *Cold smoker, apple wood dust or similar*

200g / 7oz salted butter or vegan butter
6 garlic cloves, finely chopped or grated
a bunch of parsley, finely chopped
salt and black pepper, to taste
1 large baguette

Cold smoke the butter for 2 hours (see page 83). Leave the smoked butter at room temperature to make blending easier.

Preheat the oven to 180°c (350°F). In a bowl, mash together the softened smoked butter, garlic and parsley, and season with salt and pepper to taste.

Cut deep slices into the baguette, making sure not to cut all the way through to keep it together. Spread lashings of smoked garlic butter into the gaps between the slices.

Wrap the baguette in foil and bake for 25 minutes.

Smoked carrot blinis

This is one of my favourite vegan recipes. I first tried smoked carrot as an alternative to smoked salmon at a family Christmas brunch and was blown away. I was even more surprised when I looked at the ingredients and discovered the smoky taste was made entirely from flavourings. I had to find a way to make it from scratch. Turns out, it was rather easy. Short version: get a carrot, peel it, blanch it and stick it in the smoker — a great option if you're throwing a party. Fabulous on a blini or in a salad. — JG

MAKES: *36 small blinis*
TAKES: *2 hours 45 minutes (including smoking time)*
KIT: *Cold smoker, apple wood dust or similar*

----

6 carrots peeled, then shaved into strips using peeler and blanched
150g / 5oz cashew cheese (see page 48)
    or vegan cream cheese
capers, to taste
a small bunch of dill, finely chopped
1 lemon, for squeezing
salt and black pepper, to taste

For the vegan blinis
120g / 1 cup plain flour
¼ tsp bicarbonate of soda
1 tsp baking powder
½ tsp salt
200ml / generous ¾ cup oat milk (or milk of your choice)
2 tsp caster sugar (optional but helps blinis brown)
vegetable oil, for frying

Set up your cold smoker and smoke the carrot strips for 2 hours (see page 80).

To prepare the blinis, mix all of the ingredients together in a bowl and leave to rest for 30 minutes.

Heat a frying pan with 1 teaspoon of vegetable oil. Put 2 teaspoons of batter into the pan for each blini, and fry both sides for roughly 1–2 minutes until they are golden brown.

Once the blinis have cooled, spread half a teaspoon of cashew cheese on top of each one. Top with some smoked carrot, a couple of capers and a few pieces of dill. Finish with a squeeze of lemon, a pinch of salt and a grind of black pepper.

Charred smoked sweetheart cabbage with smoked garlic aioli, capers and toasted almonds

I do this recipe all the time. It transforms the humble (and often overlooked) cabbage into the main event or a fabulous side dish. With its charred and smoky flavour, and when paired with rich smoked garlic aioli, tangy capers and crunchy toasted almonds, it takes cabbage to a whole new level, proving that even the most underrated vegetables can steal the spotlight. — JG

SERVES: *4 as a side, 2 as a main*
TAKES: *2 hours 15 minutes (including smoking time)*
KIT: *Cold smoker, apple wood dust or similar*

—

1 sweetheart cabbage
olive oil, for brushing
6 tsp capers
6 tsp toasted flaked almonds (or other nuts)
a small bunch of parsley, chopped

For the aioli
1 egg yolk
  (vegan option: use 2 tbsp aquafaba from a can of chickpeas and 2 tsp cider vinegar)
1 tsp Dijon mustard
200–300ml / ¾–1¼ cups olive oil (or you can use rapeseed oil)
2 hot smoked garlic cloves, minced or grated (see page 34)
juice of half a lemon
salt and black pepper, to taste

Cut the cabbage into 6 lengthways, keeping the core intact and the leaves together. Char for 6 minutes on each side in an oiled pan, test core is tender, then lightly coat with oil and smoke for 2 hours (see page 80).

To make the aioli, put the egg yolk and Dijon mustard in a bowl and mix well. Slowly pour the olive oil into the mixture while whisking until it thickens. If the mixture splits or curdles, save the mixture, but start again with a new egg yolk (you can add the split mixture to the new one once you have got going again). Once the aioli has thickened, add the garlic and lemon juice and season with salt and pepper.

Drizzle the aioli over the cabbage and sprinkle with capers, almonds and chopped parsley.

Smoked egg, tofu or carrot poke bowl

Sushi and poke bowls have been a permanent fixture in our kitchen for the last few years, thanks to my daughter Lucy. They are so fresh, healthy and delicious, but fun too. — JG

SERVES: *1*

TAKES: *3 hours (depending on what you are smoking)*

KIT: *Cold smoker, apple wood dust or similar*

100g / 3½oz smoked egg slices / smoked tofu chunks / smoked carrot shavings / smoked fish

150g / ¾ cup sushi rice

½ ripe avocado, chopped into cubes

10cm / 4in piece of cucumber, chopped into cubes

1 tsp pickled ginger

1 tsp black sesame seeds

a handful of edamame beans, blanched for 2 minutes

For the sushi-su

2 tbsp + 2 tsp rice wine vinegar

1 tbsp caster sugar

1 tsp salt

For the dipping sauce

2 tsp tamari

1 tsp sesame oil

1 tsp rice wine vinegar

1 small garlic clove, minced

juice of ½ lime

1 tsp maple syrup or agave syrup

black pepper

(continued overleaf)

Set up your cold smoker and smoke your chosen ingredients (see page 80–83). As well as carrots, you can use other seasonal vegetables, such as shaved courgette, steamed green beans or purple sprouting broccoli.

Rinse the sushi rice under cold water for a couple of minutes. Place the rice in a saucepan with a lid, add 180ml / ¾ cup of water and let it soak for 30 minutes. Bring the pan of rice and water to the boil, then reduce the heat to a simmer and cook with the lid on for 9 minutes.

Meanwhile, simmer the sushi-su ingredients together in a small pan until the sugar and salt have dissolved and set aside to cool. Whisk together the dipping sauce ingredients and set aside.

Once cooked, spread the rice out on a tray or a large plate to cool. As the rice cools, pour the sushi-su over it.

When the rice has cooled completely, spoon it into a large bowl. Place your poke bowl ingredients around the bowl as you like them. Drizzle the dipping sauce over the ingredients and enjoy.

Smoked cheese scones

There are few things as comforting as a warm cheesy scone out of the oven. — JG

MAKES: *8*
TAKES: *4 hours and 30 minutes (including smoking time)*
KIT: *Cold smoker, apple wood dust or similar*

—

120g / 4oz cheddar cheese
130ml / ½ cup whole milk
juice of ½ lemon
250g / 2 cups self-raising flour, plus extra for dusting
1 tsp baking powder
½ tsp salt
a pinch of chilli powder (optional)
65g / 2½oz cold unsalted butter, grated
1 egg, beaten, to glaze

Set up your cold smoker and smoke the cheddar for 4 hours (see page 82).

Preheat the oven to 200°C (400°F) and line a baking tray with baking parchment.

In a small bowl, mix the lemon juice with the milk; it will curdle, so don't worry. In a large bowl, combine the flour, baking powder, salt and chilli powder (if using) and mix well, then add the grated butter. Rub the butter into the dry ingredients using your fingertips until the mixture looks like breadcrumbs.

Grate the smoked cheddar and stir half into the bowl, then pour the curdled milk mixture into the dry ingredients and gently mix together with your hands or a knife. Handle the dough as little as possible.

(continued overleaf)

Transfer the dough to a floured work surface and bring it together until it's about 2–3cm / 1 in thick. Use a 6cm / 2½in cutter to cut out the scones, dipping the cutter in flour between each cut to stop it sticking. Bring the dough offcuts together for one not so perfect but delicious scone.

Pop on the lined baking tray, brush the tops of the scones with egg wash and then generously sprinkle with the remaining cheese. Bake in the oven for 14–15 minutes until the scones are golden brown; to check if they're cooked, tap the bottom of a scone — it should sound hollow and be golden on the bottom, too. Eat straight away with lashings of butter.

Smoked cheese scones pictured on page 112.

Smoked houmous

Always a winner and healthy too. By the way, houmous freezes really well so make an extra batch and put it in the freezer for another time. — JG

SERVES: *4*

TAKES: *2 hours 15 minutes (including smoking time)*

KIT: *Cold smoker, food processor, apple wood dust or similar*

———

240g / 8oz cooked chickpeas
  (or 1 × 400g / 14oz can chickpeas, drained)
1 large garlic clove
juice of 1½ lemons
1 tsp tahini
2 tsp water (to loosen the consistency)
2 tsp extra virgin olive oil
½ tsp ground cumin
1 tsp toasted cumin seeds
salt, to taste

Smoke the chickpeas and garlic clove in your cold smoker (see page 81), saving 2 teaspoons of whole chickpeas for the topping.

In a food processor, blitz all the ingredients except the toasted cumin seeds together. Taste and adjust the seasoning as needed, adding more salt, water or lemon juice. When it's ready, spoon into a serving dish and top with the reserved chickpeas, toasted cumin seeds and a good drizzle of olive oil.

This is delicious with crudités or in sandwiches or wraps. Try making it with cannellini beans and rosemary for something different.

Smoked cheddar arancini

There's nothing like a crispy fried snack with a cold beer or even a Negroni. This has always been one of my most popular snacks or canapés for parties and suppers. When constructing the arancini, your risotto needs to have completely cooled (either a few hours in the fridge or overnight). I'd suggest making it the day before. — JG

MAKES: *12*
TAKES: *4 hours 30 minutes (including smoking time)*
KIT: *Cold smoker, apple wood dust or similar*
—

For the risotto
2 tsp olive oil
4 tsp butter or vegan butter
1 small onion, finely diced
1 stick celery, finely diced
240g / 1¼ cups arborio rice
120ml / ½ cup white wine
1.2 litres / 5 cups hot vegetable or meat stock
80g / ⅔ cup grated Parmesan
    (or use 6 tsp nutritional yeast)
salt and black pepper, to taste

For the arancini
60g / 2½oz cheddar cheese or vegan cheese
300g / 2½ cups plain flour, seasoned with salt and pepper
3 eggs or 180ml / ¾ cup oat milk
300g / 2½ cups panko breadcrumbs
    (or homemade breadcrumbs)
1 litre / 4 cups vegetable or sunflower oil, for frying

First set up your cold smoker and smoke the cheese for the arancini for 4 hours (see page 82).

(continued overleaf)

To make the risotto, heat the oil and half the butter in a saucepan and gently sauté the onion and celery with a pinch of salt until softened, which usually takes 7–8 minutes. Add the arborio rice to the pan and stir to coat it with the oil. Pour in the white wine and cook for a couple of minutes until the liquid has evaporated. Begin adding the hot vegetable or meat stock to the rice, one ladle at a time and stir frequently. You don't want to let the risotto go dry, but you do want to keep it hot and bubbling. This step will take around 20–23 minutes. Once the rice is cooked but still slightly al dente, stir in the grated Parmesan and remaining butter. Taste and adjust the seasoning. Allow the risotto to cool, then refrigerate it for a few hours or overnight. It needs to be cold to make the arancini.

When you are ready to make the arancini, prepare three separate bowls: one with flour, one with beaten eggs or oat milk and one with breadcrumbs. Grate the smoked cheese.

Take a handful of cold, sticky risotto (around 65g / 2½oz) and form it into a ball in your hand. Make a well in the centre of the ball and place a pinch of grated cheese inside. Seal up the well and roll the rice into a ball. Repeat with the remaining risotto and cheese to make 12 balls.

To panné the arancini, first coat each ball in flour, use a spoon to dip it into the egg or milk, and finally use a different spoon to coat it in breadcrumbs. Place the coated balls on a tray.

Heat the vegetable or sunflower oil in a deep-sided pan until it reaches frying temperature (you can drop a piece of risotto in and see if it bubbles). Gently place the coated balls into the hot oil and fry on one side until golden brown, then flip to fry on the other side until nice and brown all over. Remove the arancini from the oil and place on kitchen paper to drain any excess oil, ready to munch. (Once it has cooled completely, any leftover oil can be strained and reused.)

Smoked beetroot ketchup

We often make this ketchup for weddings. It's great to include with the canapés, served alongside some crunchy, deep-fried spiced cauliflower. And of course, with a classic bacon bap (see page 117). Simple but delicious. — SD

MAKES: *Around 475ml / 2 scant cups*
TAKES: *2 hours (including smoking time)*
KIT: *Cold smoker, apple wood dust or similar*

450g / 1lb beetroot, peeled and cooked
1 tbsp rapeseed oil
½ medium white onion, diced
240ml / 1 cup apple cider vinegar
110g / ½ cup soft brown sugar
¼ tsp ground cloves
¼ tsp ground coriander
salt and black pepper, to taste

First cold smoke the beetroot for 30 minutes (see page 80).

Heat the oil in a large saucepan over a medium heat.
Add the onion and cook until soft, which usually takes around 15 minutes. Once the onion is soft, add the cooked smoked beetroot, cider vinegar, sugar, ground cloves and ground coriander to the pan. Season to taste with salt and pepper.

Allow the mixture to cool slightly to make it easier to handle, then transfer to a blender and blitz until smooth.

Chill the beetroot ketchup in the fridge before serving. It will keep in an airtight container in the fridge for up to 1 week (see photo page 116).

Classic smoked salmon

This method for dry brining and cold smoking salmon can also be used for tuna and sea trout. — SD

SERVES: *Approx. 20 people*
TAKES: *2 days (including curing and smoking time)*
KIT: *Cold smoker, oak shavings*

———

1.5kg / 3lb side of salmon, skin on
450g / 1½ cups table salt
150g / ½ cup caster (or soft brown) sugar
zest of 1 orange
zest of 1 lemon

Place the salmon on a board, skin side down, and pat it dry with kitchen paper. Mix together the salt, sugar and citrus zest and then rub this cure over the entire surface of the salmon. Transfer the salmon to a tray and cover with any remaining cure. Use a lot less cure on the thin end. Place the tray in the fridge for 12 hours, turning it once halfway through. This step is crucial for even brining.

After 12 hours, remove the salmon from the fridge and rinse off the cure under cold running water. Pat dry with kitchen paper.

Place the salmon on a clean tray and return it to the fridge overnight to allow the pellicle to form. The next day, the salmon flesh should be dry and sticky, ready for smoking.

Smoke the salmon for 12–14 hours over oak dust / chippings.

Monitor the smoking process and sample the fish periodically to determine when it has reached a level of smokiness you are happy with.

(continued overleaf)

Remember: If the temperature in the smoker goes over 25°C (77°F), it will start to cook instead of smoke. Be mindful that different parts of the smoker may have varying temperatures —we have had a piece of salmon cook in one part of the smoker and smoke beautifully on another shelf at the same time!

Smoked mussels in cider vinegar

When travelling around Ireland and looking at smokeries, I spent some time in the English market in Cork.

Frank Hederman had a stall there — he had smoked mussels in a mustard vinaigrette and I remember how good they were; as soon as I tried them, I couldn't wait to get home and have a go myself. After cold smoking, place the mussels in the fridge straight away — shellfish are high-risk ingredients, so never leave them out of the fridge for too long. — SD

SERVES: *4–6*
TAKES: *24 hours (including smoking time)*
KIT: *Cold smoker, oak shavings*

—

2 tbsp extra virgin olive oil
1kg / 2lb 4oz mussels, scrubbed and checked over
240ml / 1 cup white wine
1 small onion, finely chopped
1 small carrot, finely chopped
1 tbsp minced garlic
60ml / ¼ cup cider vinegar
1 tsp finely chopped thyme
1 tsp finely chopped rosemary
¼ tsp smoked paprika
2 tsp finely chopped chives
1 tsp finely grated orange zest
salt
1 tbsp finely chopped parsley
crusty bread and salted butter, to serve

Start by steaming open your shellfish. Heat 1 tablespoon of the oil in a large, heavy-based pot until smoking, then throw in the mussels followed by the white wine and cover with a lid.

(continued overleaf)

Cook for 2–3 minutes, just until they start to open. Using a slotted spoon, transfer the mussels to a bowl. Remove the mussels from their shells and discard any mussels that do not open. Cover the mussels and put them in the fridge. Strain the accumulated mussel juices into a separate bowl.

Lightly cold smoke the mussels over oak shavings for about 20 minutes. The mussel flesh is porous so they will not need much smoking and will hold onto the smoke well. Once smoked, put the mussels back in the fridge.

Heat the remaining olive oil in a medium saucepan and sauté the onion, carrot and garlic over a moderately low heat until softened, about 4 minutes. Add the strained mussel juices to the pan and simmer until reduced by half, about another 4 minutes. Stir in the cider vinegar, thyme, rosemary, smoked paprika, chives and orange zest and season with salt. Transfer the marinade to a bowl and refrigerate until cold, about 30 minutes.

Place the mussels into 150ml / ⅔ cup jam jars and pour the chilled marinade over them. Cover and refrigerate for at least 3 hours, and up to 24 hours.

Serve the mussels with a sprinkling of chopped parsley, crusty bread and salty butter. Pair with a glass of good Albariño or Sauvignon Blanc.

Smoky fish chowder

Save your fish trimmings or ends in the freezer until you've gathered enough to create this sensational soup. There are a number of smoked ingredients in this dish — bacon, haddock and fish trimmings — you don't have to smoke them all, but I'd recommend doing so! Leave the mussels unsmoked though; we want them to open in the chowder to add freshness and flavour. — SD

SERVES: *4–6*

TAKES: *1 hour (not including smoking time for fish)*

KIT: *Cold smoker, oak dust or chippings*

----

2 tbsp rapeseed oil

65g / 2½oz cold smoked bacon, diced (see page 117)

1 small onion, finely chopped

1 carrot, peeled and diced

1 celery stick, diced

2 sprigs of thyme

2 bay leaves

2 garlic cloves, chopped

1 tbsp plain flour

500ml / 2 cups chicken stock (homemade or bouillon)

150ml / ⅔ cup whole milk

2 tbsp sweetcorn kernels (fresh, canned or frozen)

2 large floury potatoes, peeled and diced

300g / 10oz cold smoked haddock, skinned and cut into 3–4cm / 1½in cubes

200g / 7oz mussels, cleaned and checked

75ml / 5 tbsp double cream

a pinch of cayenne pepper

200g / 7oz cold smoked fish trimmings (salmon, mackerel etc), diced

(continued overleaf)

salt and black pepper, to taste
a good handful of parsley, chopped
juice of 1 lemon
freshly grated nutmeg, to finish

If you're starting from scratch with your smoked fish, rather than using up leftovers, prepare it by using the general dry brine recipe: 3 measures of table salt to 1 measure of caster sugar (see page 26). Cover and leave in the fridge for 20 mins to cure. Rinse off the brine and place back in the fridge overnight to fully dry out. Put your cured fish in the cold smoker for 8–10 hours.

Heat the oil in a large saucepan and fry the lardons until crisp and golden. Add the onion, carrot, celery, thyme and bay leaves and cook very gently until softened. This will take a good 10 minutes so be very patient! Add the garlic and cook for a few more minutes, then stir in the flour and cook for a couple of minutes. Gradually add the chicken stock, stirring constantly, followed by the milk, sweetcorn and diced potatoes. Simmer until the potatoes are almost cooked, the carrots are soft, and the sauce has thickened slightly.

Add the cubes of smoked haddock and the mussels. Cover the pan and cook over a low heat until the fish is just cooked and the mussels have opened (discard any mussels that haven't opened). Stir in the cream, cayenne pepper, salt and pepper to taste, smoked fish trimmings and bring back up to a simmer. Finally, add the chopped parsley and lemon juice. Ladle into warm bowls and finish with some grated nutmeg. Serve with some crusty bread or some of Jen's smoked cheese scones (see page 99).

Smoked pork fillet

My classic dry brine recipe below can also be used when cold smoking lamb loin, duck breast and venison loin to make charcuterie. — SD

SERVES: *5*

TAKES: *2½ days (including curing and smoking time)*

KIT: *Cold smoker, oak chippings*

———

500g / 1lb 2oz pork fillet
60g / 2½oz table salt
40g / 1½oz soft dark brown sugar
15g / 3 tsp toasted fennel seeds, crushed
15g / 3tsp freshly ground black pepper

Lay the pork fillet out on a board. Mix together the salt, sugar, fennel seeds and black pepper to make a dry brine, then rub this all over the surface of the pork. Place the pork on a tray and cover with any remaining cure, then place in the fridge for 24 hours.

After curing, wash off the cure from the meat and pat it dry with kitchen paper. Place the meat back in the fridge for another 24 hours to dry out and create a sticky pellicle. Cold smoke the meat for 14 hours over oak chippings (see page 84). These instructions serve as guidelines; adjust the smoking time according to your preference.

Brilliant bacon bap

My favourite way of enjoying cured, smoked pork: crispy bacon on good sourdough with the kids on a Sunday morning.

You can always tell when shop-bought bacon has been wet brined: it's bland, flabby, and lots of moisture comes out when you cook it. Dry brining bacon at home will give you a far superior product that is simple to make and tastes better. Pork belly is ideal for making streaky bacon and is the easiest to cure because it has a consistent thickness. Pork loin will make back bacon, but this is harder to cure because a larger loin can have uneven widths across the meat.

In this recipe, we use maple and juniper to flavour the dry brine, but you could use anything (as long as you use the basic cure ratio: 1kg meat: 250g cure); try thyme and rosemary, chilli and garlic, star anise, or even seaweed! — SD

SERVES: *3–4*
TAKES: *6 days (includes 5 days to cure and ½ day to smoke)*
KIT: *Cold smoker and oak, maple or hickory chippings*

For the bacon
1kg / 2lb 4oz pork loin or belly pork (with or without rind)
75g / 3oz cure salt / sodium nitrate (see page 26)
75g / 3oz coarse sea salt
6 juniper berries, smashed
40g / 1½oz soft light brown sugar
50g / 2oz maple syrup

For the bacon baps
8 rashers cold smoked streaky bacon
2 large floury white baps, cut in half
lashings of salted butter
condiment of your choice

(continued overleaf)

Place the meat on a board and pat it dry with kitchen paper. Mix together the sodium nitrate, coarse sea salt, juniper berries, sugar and maple syrup to make the dry brine, then rub this all over the meat. Transfer the meat to a heavy-duty freezer or ziplock bag with any remaining cure and squeeze out all the air. Place the bag on a tray and refrigerate for 5 days for belly or 6 days for loin (as belly is thinner than loin). Turn the meat daily to ensure an even cure.

After curing, remove the meat from the bag, wash off the cure, and pat it dry with kitchen paper. Place the cured meat on a clean tray and leave in the fridge overnight to let the pellicle form.

The next day, the flesh should be dry and sticky ready for smoking. Smoke the meat for 12–14 hours over oak chippings (see page 84).

To make your bacon baps, grill the bacon until wonderful and crispy on both sides. Meanwhile, spread lots of cold salted butter on both sides of the bap. Place the hot crispy bacon inside and eat it straight away, with a condiment of your choice. I'd highly recommend beetroot ketchup! (See recipe on page 105).

Smoked bacon and black bean soup

Soup of the day is a restaurant kitchen staple. When I worked as a chef in London and New York, we'd often use ingredients like bacon trimmings or ham hock. I discovered the hearty goodness of black beans when I was in America. So I combined the ingredients to create this comforting smoky soup. — SD

SERVES: *8*

TAKES: *2 hours 30 minutes (not including curing and smoking the bacon)*

KIT: *Cold smoker and oak, maple or hickory chippings*

----

1 tbsp rapeseed oil
2 onions, finely chopped
1 celery stick, finely chopped
1 large carrot, peeled and finely chopped
6 garlic cloves, finely chopped
2 bay leaves
a small bunch of coriander, stalks and leaves
    chopped separately
2 tbsp ground cumin
1 tbsp ground coriander
1 jalapeño, finely chopped (seeds included)
250g / 9oz black beans, soaked in water overnight
    (enough to cover the beans and a further 5cm / 2in
    above, then keep the water for later in the recipe)
500g / 1lb 2oz cold smoked bacon belly (see page 117)
Greek yoghurt, to serve

For the salsa
1 mango, finely diced
1 jalapeño, deseeded and finely chopped
40g / 1½oz coriander, finely chopped

(continued overleaf)

1 tbsp olive oil
zest of 1 lime, plus 1 tbsp juice
salt and black pepper, to taste

Mix all the salsa ingredients together, season to taste and set aside.

Heat the oil in a large saucepan and fry the onion, celery, carrot, garlic, bay leaves and chopped coriander stalks until they are soft. Stir in the spices and jalapeño.

Add the black beans, bacon and the bean soaking water to the pan. (Normally you wouldn't use this water, but we use it here for flavour and also colour. It's completely safe — trust me, I have eaten enough of it!)

Bring to the boil and skim off any scum that forms on the surface — this is important as it takes away any impurities. Continue doing this as the soup cooks for about 2 hours, stirring occasionally so that the soup does not stick.

Once the beans are soft, remove the pan from the heat and take out the bacon and bay leaves. Blitz the soup in a blender until it reaches a thick, smooth consistency. Season as you go, but keep in mind bacon is salty, so you won't need much.

Chop the bacon into lardons, then bring the soup back up to the boil and add the bacon bits. Ladle the soup into bowls and top each with salsa, yoghurt and the reserved coriander leaves.

Smoked pork rillettes with pickles and crusty bread

I first tried pork rillettes when I was working at the Mirabelle restaurant in London. Every day we ran a 'de jour' menu, which usually had some sort of rillettes — whether it was duck, pork, salmon or wild boar. I found it so simple, yet really tasty and satisfying... rich too! When I set up cnwd, a smoker and charcuterie business, I knew that we needed to do something similar. We were buying woodland-reared pork from a farm in Whitland and we had a smoker, too. Why not try smoking the pork? When we launched, the locals weren't too familiar with rillettes (it's more of a French thing), but it went down a storm and became one of our bestsellers. When we took it to London, both Harrods and Fortnum & Mason's food buyers were blown away and were some of the first to take it.— SD

SERVES: *4–6*
TAKES: *2–3 hours, followed by 2–3 days in the fridge*
KIT: *Cold smoker and oak, maple or hickory chippings*
NOTE: *In this recipe the pork isn't brined first. It is smoked for flavour rather than preservation. The fat that the pork is set with in the jar preserves it.*

———

1kg / 2lb 4oz large pork belly, diced
1 tbsp sunflower oil
1 large onion, diced
50g / 2oz garlic purée
2 tsp salt
2 tsp chopped thyme
1 tsp ground black pepper
300ml / 1¼ cups white wine

(continued overleaf)

Leave your diced pork belly in the fridge overnight on a wire rack to dry out or pat dry with kitchen paper.

To cold smoke, put the pork in the smoker for 2 hours. Any more than that it would be too smoky as the smoke sticks to the fat really easily. We use oak, but maple and hickory would also lend themselves well to the pork.

Heat the oil in a large heavy-based saucepan over a medium heat. Sweat the onion until tender, then add the garlic, salt, thyme and pepper. Increase the heat to high and add the pork belly. Fry until the meat has coloured slightly, then pour in the white wine and reduce the heat so it is gently bubbling. Cook the pork belly with the lid on until tender and the meat falls apart. This will take approx. 2 hours. Skim off any residue from the surface throughout the cooking.

Sterilise small jars, Kilner jars or Mason jars along with their lids by boiling them in water or steaming them at 100°C (200°F).

Skim off most of the fat from the pork belly into a plastic jug and set it aside.

Half-fill the bowl of a food processor with the pork and, using the pulse mode, begin to pulse and break down the meat to a coarse, flaky consistency. Season to taste.

Fill each of the sterilised jars with the pork mixture and seal by covering with roughly 3mm / ⅛in of the reserved fat. It is important that there is no meat protruding out of the fat as this is protecting it. Seal the jars tightly with their lids, ensuring they are dry before closing.

Place the sealed jars in the fridge and leave for 2–3 days. They will keep for up to 3 months. Once opened, consume within 3 days. Serve with crusty bread, butter and wholegrain mustard and cornichons.

Smoked venison loin with celeriac remoulade

We have a gamekeeper local to us who culls the Dinefwr estate venison in Llandeilo. The venison on this estate is fallow, which are a smaller breed not native to the British Isles but believed to have been brought over by the Normans and William the Conqueror. Fallow deer is a good entry level venison meat if you are not used to it as the meat is not too powerful and gamey. — SD

SERVES: *4*
TAKES: *12 hours for curing and smoking; 1 day for pickling*
KIT: *Cold smoker and oak chippings*

400g / 14oz venison loin
7 tbsp good-quality mayonnaise (or make your own)
3 tbsp Dijon mustard
3 tbsp + 1 tsp hazelnut oil
2 tbsp chives, chopped
1 tbsp finely chopped shallot
1 tsp sherry vinegar
1 small celeriac (about 650g / 1lb 7oz)
toast and watercress, to serve
100g / 3½oz toasted hazelnuts, to garnish
salt and black pepper, to taste

For the pickled blackberries
125ml / ½ cup white wine vinegar
4 tbsp water
60g / ¼ cup caster sugar
¼ tsp salt
200g / 7oz blackberries
1 star anise

(continued overleaf)

Prepare your dry brine using the general recipe on page 26 (1 measure table salt: 1 measure soft brown sugar, option to add some chopped dried juniper berries). Sprinkle the cure evenly over the venison loin, cover and leave in the fridge for 36 hours. Wash off the cure and place the venison back in the fridge overnight on a wire rack to dry out. Then cold smoke your cured venison for 12 hours.

To make the pickled blackberries, start by gently heating the white wine vinegar, water, sugar and salt in a small saucepan until fully dissolved. Allow the mixture to cool. Add the fruit to a jar or container and cover with the cooled liquid. Leave for a day until you achieve the desired taste, and then store in the fridge for up to a month.

Next, in a large bowl, mix together the mayonnaise, mustard, hazelnut oil, chives, shallot and sherry vinegar. Season generously with salt and pepper.

Peel and quarter the celeriac, then quickly cut it into matchsticks before tossing it into the sauce (celeriac discolours on interaction with oxygen).

Cut the smoked venison into thin slices and serve with the celeriac remoulade, toast, watercress and pickled blackberries. Finish with a sprinkling of toasted hazelnuts. Enjoy with a Merlot or Cabernet Sauvignon.

Smoked game bird pie

Combining the rich flavours of game meat and the subtle
flavours of oak smoke in an irresistible pastry crust, you'll
find photos on pages 88 and 137. Delicious.— SD

SERVES: *6–8*
TAKES: *4 hours (including smoking and chilling time)*
KIT: *Cold smoker, oak chippings*
—

4 skinless pheasant breast fillets
4 skinless partridge breast fillets
2 skinless pigeon breast fillets
25g / 1oz plain flour, plus extra for rolling out
olive oil
50g / 2oz cold smoked streaky bacon (see page 117)
250g / 9oz button mushrooms, quartered
3 carrots, peeled and diced
3 garlic cloves, chopped
1 medium onion, finely chopped
½ leek, trimmed, diced
1 tsp thyme leaves
200ml / generous ¾ cup dry white wine
500ml / 2 cups chicken stock
150ml / ⅔ cup milk
150ml / ⅔ cup double cream
1 tbsp chopped tarragon
375g / 13oz ready-rolled puff pastry
1 egg yolk, beaten
salt and black pepper, to taste

Cold smoke the un-brined breasts of meat for 2 hours over
oak chippings (see page 78). This is a fairly quick recipe, not
charcuterie. We are just adding a slightly smoky flavour to

a classic pie dish, rather than the curing/smoking being the main processing of the meat.

Dice the meat into roughly 1cm / ½in pieces. Put the flour in a tray and season with salt and pepper, then dust the meat.

Place a large saucepan with a lid over a medium-high heat, then add a little oil. Once hot, add as much meat as will fit in a single layer (you don't want to overcrowd the pan). Fry until golden brown and set aside. Do this in roughly three batches, adding extra oil when needed.

Add the pancetta to the pan and fry until light brown, then add the mushrooms, carrots, garlic, onion, leek and thyme and fry until all the vegetables are soft. Pour the white wine into the pan and cook until it reduces almost completely, then add the stock, milk and cream and bring to a simmer. Stir occasionally to prevent sticking.

Lower the pan heat, then return the meat pieces (along with any juices) to the pan. Season to taste. Cover and cook for 40 minutes – 1 hour, stirring occasionally. If the mixture gets too thick, add a splash of milk to loosen it. Stir in the tarragon. When the meat is tender (and keep in mind game birds take longer to cook than chicken), transfer to a deep pie dish.

Unroll the pastry and cut out a shape a little bigger than the pie dish. Brush the rim with beaten egg, then cover the dish with the pastry lid, pressing down the edges. Trim any excess pastry and create a small hole or X in the middle of the pie lid to allow steam to escape when cooking.

Place the pie in the fridge for 20 minutes to chill. Preheat the oven to 200°C (400°F). Glaze the top of the pie with the remaining egg, then place it on a baking tray in the oven for about 30 minutes, or until the pastry is golden brown. Serve with mashed swede and seasonal greens. Enjoy!

Smoked panna cotta

While playing around with the cold smoker, I tried smoking cream once and couldn't believe the results. I've always been a big fan of panna cotta as it's such a crowd-pleaser, so I had to try it with the smoked cream. Then, because of the smokiness of the cream, I thought it would be fabulous with a more caramel taste — hence the brown sugar. I hope you enjoy it as much as we do. — JG

SERVES: *4*
TAKES: *24 hours (including smoking and setting time)*
KIT: *Cold smoker, apple wood dust or similar*

———

300ml / 1¼ cups double cream
2 gelatine leaves (each about 2g)
110g soft brown sugar
150ml / ⅔ cup whole milk
1 tsp vanilla extract (or seeds from ½ vanilla pod)
shortbread and seasonal berries, to serve

Cold smoke the double cream for 2 hours (see page 83).

Soak the gelatine leaves in cold water until they become soft.

In a saucepan, gently heat the smoked cream with the sugar until the sugar dissolves and bubbles start to form around the edge of the pan. Remove the pan from the heat, then squeeze the softened gelatine leaves to remove excess water and add them to the cream mixture; stir until dissolved. Add the milk and vanilla to the mixture and stir until well combined.

Pour the mixture into 4 panna cotta moulds or small metal dishes. Refrigerate for at least 4 hours or overnight until set.

To serve, fill a bowl with 3cm / 1in boiling water. Dip each panna cotta mould into the hot water for 10 seconds to loosen the edges. Place an upturned plate on top of the mould, hold the plate firmly against the dish and flip it over together so the plate is the right way up. Take the mould away, et voilà! Serve with shortbread and your choice of seasonal berries, fruit or coulis.

Smoked pear and chocolate tart

I've always baked — at home as a kid with my mum and all through my life. I believe many things can be solved with a slice of something sweet and a good chat. I love a good tart as a dessert and, in my research, smoking the pear, chocolate and butter was a revelation to me. I was blown away by the result. If you only smoke one item, make it the butter; it's a game changer! — JG

SERVES: *8*
TAKES: *3 hours (including smoking and chilling time)*
KIT: *Cold smoker, apple wood dust or similar*

—

For the pastry
150g / 5oz unsalted butter
250g / 2 cups plain flour
1 tbsp caster sugar
a pinch of salt
2 eggs

For the frangipane
125g / 4½oz unsalted butter
95g / ½ cup caster sugar
3 eggs
125g / 1¼ cups ground almonds
200g / 7oz cold smoked dark chocolate
a pinch of salt
2 pears
thick double cream, to serve

First, cold smoke the butter and chocolate and hot smoke the pears (see pages 83 and 34). Slice the pears into eight pieces and set to one side.

Dice the cold smoked butter and add to a mixing bowl with the plain flour and combine until the mixture resembles breadcrumbs. Add the caster sugar, salt and 1 of the eggs and mix until just combined. Bring together to form a dough.

Take a 23cm / 9in loose-bottomed tart tin. Roll out the pastry on a floured surface to form a circle that is 2cm / ¾in bigger than the tart tin. Line the tin with the pastry, pressing it into the edges and crimping the top. Prick the base with a fork and refrigerate for 30 minutes.

Preheat the oven to 180°c (350°F). Line the pastry with baking parchment and fill with baking beans. Bake the pastry for 25 minutes, then remove the baking beans and parchment. Beat the remaining egg, then brush the pastry with egg wash and bake for an additional 10 minutes.

While the pastry is baking, melt the cold smoked chocolate in a dish over hot water and set aside. Cream together the smoked butter and caster sugar for the frangipane. Gradually add the eggs, then mix in the ground almonds, melted cold smoked chocolate and a pinch of salt. Once the pastry is baked, fill it with the frangipane mixture, then arrange the hot smoked pear slices on top. Bake the tart for 30 minutes, or until the filling is set. Serve with double cream.

Smoked pear and chocolate tart pictured overleaf.

Epilogue

Smoking food at home is a new and exciting skill for the curious cook to learn. And in an ever-changing world where many of us are starting to eat less meat and fish, smoking takes vegetables, fruits, cheese, nuts and more to a whole new level; giving us plenty of options in the pursuit of a varied, sustainable diet.

We hope we have opened the door for you to experiment with different foods and different methods of smoking. For us, having a day at home filling a cold or hot smoker and playing around with different brines, types of wood chippings and fresh ingredients is a day well spent. So, we'd encourage you to get started then keep practising, tasting, refining — and having fun.

Perhaps you'll go on to build a cold smoker for your outside space (it doesn't have to be big!) and smoke pieces of cheese or salmon to give as gifts. Or maybe you can even share what you have learnt with others. In our opinion, there is nothing better than sitting down with friends or family and sharing a homemade — and home-smoked — meal. Enjoy!

About the authors

Scott Davis has been taught by and worked for the best: Marco Pierre White, Nobu Maksuhisa, Gordon Ramsay, Gary Rhodes and Jean-Georges Vongerichten in New York. He has learnt his trade the hard way by working with the people with the highest, and most exacting standards. It was under the arches at London's Mirabelle restaurant that Scott first 'smoked' and this experience ignited a lifelong passion for smoked foods. Later he explored artisan smokehouses around the British Isles, before returning home to Wales to create his own dishes in his own way. Together with his partner, Kirsty, he runs Strawberry Shortcake, a bespoke catering company based in Carmarthen.

Jen Goss lives on a smallholding in west Wales with her family, following a lifelong dream to live by the sea and work the land. The produce of Jen's land and surrounding hedgerows provides ample supplies for Our Two Acres — the catering company she set up after a career in the hospitality industry in London. In 2016, she co-authored *Do Preserve* with Anja Dunk and Mimi Beaven. Jen is currently working on a project called Cook 24, funded by the Shared Prosperity Fund, teaching children, schools and communities how to cook, where our food comes from, and how we can change the current poverty and obesity crisis through food education.

Index

INDEX

Books in the series

Also available

Available in print, digital and audio formats from booksellers or via our
website: **thedobook.co**. To hear about events and forthcoming titles,
find us on social media **@dobookco**, or subscribe to our newsletter.